Serving
as
SENDERS

Serving as Senders is formatted for individual and group study. The eight study sessions have sections on:
- *For Your Personal Involvement*
- *Action steps*
- *Group Discussion*
- *For Further Action*

Serving as Senders is also available as a six-hour live seminar. Contact Emmaus Road, International, 7150 Tanner Court, San Diego CA 92111 USA. (619) 292-7020

Serving
as
SENDERS

Neal Pirolo

Emmaus Road, International
7150 Tanner Court   San Diego, CA 92111   (619) 292-7020

Scripture quotations are paraphrases by the author.

The opening stories in Chapters Four and Five are adapted from *In Other Words* January 1977 and October 1990 issues respectively and are used by permission from Wycliffe Bible Translators. Materials in Chapter Eight are from "Catch the Vision" brochure (IFMA) and the *Catch the Vision 2000* book (Bethany House Publishers, 1991) used by permission.

Published by Emmaus Road, International
7150 Tanner Court, San Diego, California 92111

Printed in the United States of America
ISBN 1-880185-00-8

Dedication

To the many
cross-cultural workers
and their support teams
out of whose experiences
come the pages of this book.

Acknowledgements

Who would have thought such a little book would bring such labor? Yet who would have thought of the joy it also brings? The coaching team was great! The first acknowledgement must go to the Holy Spirit, our inspiration and comfort. Second, to my wife Yvonne who often critiqued and rewrote so forcefully that I tried to get her name on the cover. To my brother Paul who didn't laugh when he read through the first draft and used his editing skills to meticulously comb through the final manuscript. To Alice Lovas who coordinated and wrote much of the Sacramento church's case study. To the friends of El Adobe Trust who funded the first printing. And even to our kids, for, as our son Byron pointed out, our experiences in raising them have built into us what it took to stay with this project to its completion!

And finally and foremost, "unto Him who is able to do exceeding abundantly above all that we can ask or think; unto Him be glory throughout all ages" (Ephesians 3:20).

Contents

Preface

I sat in the upper level of the auditorium at the University of Illinois in Urbana, listening to the heavyweights of the evangelical community challenge 17,000 college students to a vital and personal commitment to world evangelization. It was InterVarsity's Urbana Student Mission Conference.

I must admit I had begun daydreaming when all of a sudden there was that statement: "In secular war, for every one person on the battle front, there are *nine* others backing him up in what is called the 'line of communication.'"

The concept exploded like a mortar shell! The speaker had been drawing a parallel between secular war and the spiritual warfare that accompanies cross-cultural ministry. He continued, "And how can we expect to win with any less than that ratio? God is not looking for Lone Rangers or Superstars; He is commanding an army—soldiers of the Cross."

I said, "Thank You, Lord, for that confirmation!" At that time I was directing a one-year school of evangelism which had a strong emphasis on cross-cultural outreach. Though I had had no background in secular war, as soon as students applied to the school, I had been encouraging them to build around themselves a team of *nine* people who would support them in prayer, since enrolling in this school was saying to the enemy, "I am getting out of the *pew* and onto the *battlefield!*"

Since that evening at Urbana, with more vigor than ever I have encouraged, exhorted—even implored—

anyone going into cross-cultural outreach ministry to not leave home without a strong, committed support team—a group that accepts the ministry of serving as senders.

By the time we're through with our study together, you'll be able to answer this question: How can I get involved in the Great Commission of world evangelization even though I'm just an ordinary human being called to stay at home?

You can become personally involved in the mission process as a sender.

Ministering by His grace,
Neal Pirolo
San Diego, California

Chapter One   The Need for Senders

"And how shall they [go] preach except they are sent?"
Romans 10:15

"Beth! Wake up! Please, Beth! Wake up!" Beth's roommate held the empty Valium bottle in her hand and knew Beth wouldn't wake up. But instinct said to get help. The people in the next apartment helped her carry Beth to the car. A mile that seemed half way around the world brought them to the hospital. They pumped Beth's stomach. She stirred and opened her eyes.

Months later Beth could talk about it:

"I had had a normal life before this. Friends, a loving family, a good church life. Basically, I was a happy person. I had been a professional for ten years. I had held reputable positions. I had managed people. And I had managed myself quite well...until this.

"I had just returned from a six-month missionary venture in the Orient. My feelings were running rampant. Nostalgia flooded me as I remembered the good times; nightmares and flashbacks haunted me in the quiet solitude of night. Nobody was interested; nobody had time to hear what I had to say.

"I had just come from a fruitful experience as an administrative assistant in a medical clinic. Dumped back into the busy lifestyle of metropolitan Washington, D.C., I lost all sense of identity. Deepening feelings of isolation caused me to withdraw all the more.

"I thought if I got back into my work I could refocus my life. But the emotional instability mounted. One nightmare kept recurring:

"We had been in a village doing some medical work. Through the thundering of a tropical storm, I awoke to the sound of gunfire. Before I could go back to sleep, I saw them dragging the body of a man past the doorway of my hut. The story was that he had been caught in the fields stealing opium.

"Now back in D.C., I would awaken at night to the sounds in my brain of the *pow-pow* of the guns. And the whole ugly scene would flash through my mind again. I began using tranquilizers to control my instability. But before seven or eight in the evening, I was lost in anxiety, confusion, uncertainty—crying uncontrollably.

"Conversely, I also had a sense of 'special' knowledge. I was fulfilled by a good missionary experience. Hadn't I *been there*? Hadn't I been successful? Hadn't I bonded with and nurtured Billy to health?

"We had been on our way home from some medical work in the hill country. Along the trail I stumbled on this three-month-old infant. His hands and feet were bound together with rope. He was addicted to opium. He was almost dead. We inquired as best we could whose son he was. His mother already had four children under the age of five.

"The man who was thought to be the father was away on 'business' three to four weeks at a time. It is probably this woman who had left him there to die. A couple hundred yards away was an abandoned hut. We said we would wait there until nighttime to talk with his mother. She never came. At the clinic we were able to give him the care needed. We called him Billy, and he was eventually adopted by a local Christian doctor.

"I became hyper-vigilant about this great need out there. I felt a lot of anger toward people who wouldn't let me talk about my experiences. My pastor wouldn't let me share at church. No Sunday school class had the time for me. My parents couldn't show enough interest to even look at my pictures. I became judgmental and condemning: 'How can you be thinking about buying a new car when there are such great needs out there?' But I couldn't say any of that out loud. Hurt, fear, anger and guilt all turned inward in severe depression. I couldn't sleep at night; I couldn't get out of bed in the morning. I quit my job. I took more and more tranquilizers. *I just wanted somebody to acknowledge that I was back home!*

"One Sunday morning after church, I gathered the strength to again go to my pastor and say, 'I am at the end of my rope! I think I'm losing it! I need your help!' With his arm around me, he said, 'Beth, I am busy. I am so tied up this week. But if you must, call my office to set an appointment for a week from Wednesday. Beth, if you would just get into the Word more....'

"Through the dazed fog of an existence I had been living in, all of a sudden it became crystal clear: 'Pastor, I'm not worth your time!' I had made other desperate calls to various counselors. One guy tried to date me. A psychiatrist had given my condition a fancy label. But now it was clear: 'I'm not worth anybody's time!'

"I decided to take the rest of the bottle of Valium."

It would astound most Christians to hear missionaries honestly express their desperate need for support in one area or another. Most pleas aren't as dramatic as Beth's. But each speaks of a personal need for those who will come alongside them and serve as senders.

Missions does not just focus on those who go. Those who serve as senders are equally significant.

A Biblical Foundation

If anybody knew about going on missionary journeys *and* needing a support team, it was the Apostle Paul. He said, "...and how can they [go] preach except they are *sent?*" In Romans chapter ten, he established the vitality of cross-cultural outreach on these two levels of involvement: *Those who go* and *those who serve as senders.*

Paul first quoted Joel: "For whosoever shall call upon the name of the Lord shall be saved." Then, in clear linear logic so well understood by the Roman mind, he appealed: "How then shall they call on Him in whom they have not believed? And how shall they believe in Him of whom they have not heard?"

Today's estimate is that 2.5 billion people have not had a culturally relevant presentation of the Gospel.

"And how shall they hear without a *preacher?*" Yes, there must be a "preacher"—the missionary, the cross-cultural worker, the *one who goes.* By whatever name and by whatever means he gets there, there must be a proclaimer of the Good News. God chose it to be this way. (Throughout our study, we'll be referring to your missionary with a generic "he"—though at all times we mean *he, she* or *they!*)

Today's estimate is that there are worldwide 285,250 career foreign missionaries and 180,000 short term missionaries.

But wait. There is one more question in this series: "And how shall they preach except they are *sent?*" (Romans 10:13-15). Paul acknowledged that there are others besides those who go who must be involved in this worldwide evangelization endeavor: those who are serving as senders.

Those who go and those who serve as senders are like two units on the same cross-cultural outreach team. Both are equally important. Both are vitally involved in the fulfillment of the Great Commission. Both are dynamically integrated and moving toward the same goal. And both are assured success, for those in God's work are on the winning team!

From the humble beginnings of one hundred young people at the Mount Hermon Meeting of 1886, the Student Volunteer Movement identified and fielded over 20,000 men and women to be *goers*—ones set apart to declare the Gospel and teachings of Christ to a lost and dying world.

This same movement mobilized an army in excess of 80,000 mission-minded people who pledged themselves to stay at home and support those who went.

In decades past, many grew up in mission-minded churches. Men and women from faraway places came to speak of the challenge to follow in their steps. Most of the time it was easy to understand that the two squads on the missionary team were *those who go* and *those who say, "Goodbye!"*

Maybe some people in your fellowship want to be involved in world evangelization but don't feel called to go right now. The good news is there's more they can do than just say goodbye!

There is a tremendous need for *senders.* And the need goes far beyond the traditional token involvement of showing up for a farewell party or writing out a check to missions. A cross-cultural worker needs the support of a team of people while he is preparing to go, while he is on the field and when he returns home.

A careful reading of Paul's missionary letters will reveal how much time he spent talking to his support team—those who were involved with him in the ministry. Sometimes he complimented them, sometimes he expressed his loneliness in being away from them, sometimes he exhorted and challenged them. But he always thanked God for them.

A support team of senders is just as critical to a missionary today. Let's look at some very good reasons why.

A Cross-Cultural Worker's Life Time-line

Consider this diagram of the physical/emotional/ mental/spiritual life time-line of a cross-cultural worker during his missionary experience.

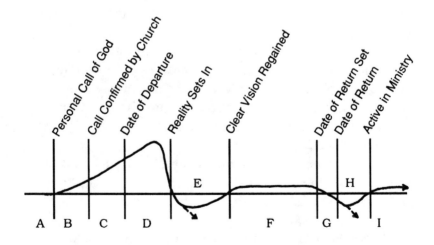

A Cross-Cultural Worker's
Life Time-line

A. "Normal" Living

The flat, horizontal line of this diagram represents the "normal living" base line of your missionary's existence before he even had a thought about missions. This is not to say that his life was flat! There were normal ups and downs, but for the purpose of comparison, consider the line as his *normal* life before missions.

The line that resembles the dips and curves of a roller coaster ride is the changing pulse of your missionary's entire being as he passes through his missionary experience. One veteran said about the ups and downs of missionary life: "Missionary living takes me on a trip that is totally outside the realm of every comfort zone I have come to enjoy!"

The vertical lines indicate segments of time, mileposts along his missionary venture. The relative spaces between the lines may vary due to many factors. But these are expected phases of which you, his support person, should be aware. As you are giving your support, anticipate the next milepost of your cross-cultural worker's life time-line. And be available to offer your assistance.

B. Anticipation of Approval

At some point, your missionary emerged from his closet of prayer, having grappled with all the normal feelings of inadequacy. Want to know how he probably felt? Read through Exodus chapters three and four to hear the patriarch Moses rehearse his five excuses of inadequacy. While you're there, notice that God answers each of his protests with *His* all-sufficiency. Boldly or with some reluctance, your friend announced that he believed God had placed a personal call on his life to become a missionary. Every fiber of his being has undergone a rise in excitement and apprehension, visions of grandeur and nightmares of depression.

C. Anticipation of Departure

The day finally comes: The church, mission board or other responsible body (see Acts 13:1-4) has confirmed that personal call with their approval. It has been determined that your missionary is really going! Through days, weeks, even months of preparation, support-team building, and training, anticipation heightens as the date of departure draws near.

D. Honeymoon Period

Your missionary is catapulted into space in a jetliner, but his emotions are flying ten feet above the plane. The "honeymoon" has begun. For a period of time he moves around in a protective bubble, enjoying all of the quaint newnesses. Even the single control on the shower that produces only cold water is "interesting." There is so much to observe, to take in. It's all so...different!

E. Culture Stress

The time that passes between these identified stages will vary according to circumstances. But as surely as night follows day, this next stage is inevitable. One morning your missionary rudely awakens to the reality that the single handle will *never* produce hot water! He realizes he has committed himself to circumstances that are no longer quaint; they are now *weird*, even *barbaric!*

The adventure of discovery has turned to the dread of "What's next?" The first bugs of dysentery keep him up all night. The fact that this is the most difficult language in the world to learn has him looking for a permanent interpreter. The first hints of persecution or the awareness that people are not going to change as easily or as rapidly as he had hoped have him asking God to "Let this cup pass from me...." The pinnacles of ecstasy have plummeted to the depths of despair. Culture stress has set in.

Most missionaries don't want to talk about this stage of missionary life because the people back home won't think of them as "spiritual" enough if they admit to some of these trying times. It is at this time that your cross-cultural worker needs your support. Many—too many—crash here. Of course, some turn back before they leave the airport!

F. Ministry of Love

But your missionary has been taught that culture stress is a normal stage to go through. Therefore, he will do just that: Go through it into a beautiful time of ministry motivated by the love of Christ. Because of your strong support he will emerge with a strengthened vision of God's purposes in his life and his reasons for being a missionary. All is not rosy. The adversaries are there. But the "great, effectual open doors" of ministry that Paul talked about are there, too (see 1 Corinthians 16:9).

G. Anticipation of Return

Life goes on. As surely as this missionary journey had a starting point, the time will come when your cross-cultural worker will, like Paul's team, "sail back to Antioch from where we had been recommended by the grace of God for the work which we have now completed" (Acts 14:26).

Again, his feelings are mixed. Yes, your missionary wants to come home to see you. But he has made new friends. He has new ideas and ideals. He has changed behavior patterns that he knows will be difficult to integrate into his new home environment. No, he isn't returning to his old home environment when he comes back. For you also have changed!

His heart has been broken with compassion for the lost; and there are so few to take his place in ministry. The desire to stay and continue in ministry usually outweighs the desire to return home. Thus, the emotional/psychological/spiritual pulse of your missionary drops again.

Probably the shortest letter ever written was to a missionary whose furlough time had been scheduled; all plans had been set. Then, remembering the difficulties of previous times back in the States, he wrote that he had changed his mind; he was not coming. The reply came back: "Pete! Get home!" He came and his support team was able to help him through the next stage.

H. Culture Stress in Reverse

In Chapter Seven, we deal extensively with the support your cross-cultural worker needs after his return. The trauma to his entire being during re-entry is intense. An example is the re-entry desperation of Beth who told her story at the beginning of this chapter. In this great time of need, your missionary might feel especially inadequate to do any thing about it.

During this time of reverse culture stress, coming back home mandates strong support.

I. Full Integration

A missionary who has been trained to anticipate the stress of coming home and has a strong re-entry support team will, in time, fully integrate his changed self into the changed home environment. He will be a positive change-agent in his church and community. He will "abide a long time with the disciples there" (Acts 14:28). He will, like Paul, "continue in Antioch, teaching and preaching the Word" (Acts 15:35). And who knows? After a while he might even say, "Hey, Barnabas, let's go out again!" (See Acts 15:36.)

Today no cross-cultural worker should leave home without a strong, integrated, educated, knowledgeable, excited-as-he-is, active team of people who have committed themselves to the work of serving as senders.

You may be a part of that team. Your heart is stirred by people of other cultures, yet you have not heard His call to go. When a missionary speaks at your church or a breakthrough is reported, there is a special quickening in your pulse. Yet you know God has directed you to stay at home. You may be called to the ministry of serving as a sender.

Prayerfully consider serving as a sender in any one or more of six areas of support:

Moral Support—just "being there"

Logistics Support—all the bits and pieces

Financial Support—money, money, money

Prayer Support—spiritual warfare at its best

Communication Support—letters, tapes and more

Re-entry Support—more than applauding the safe landing of his jumbo jet

Each area has its unique responsibilities; each is best served by specific gifts within the Body of Christ. Allow His Spirit to speak to your heart about your possible involvement in one of these phases of support.

God's *call* on your life to serve as a sender must be just as vibrant as the call on the life of the one you send. Likewise, the *commitment* you make must be as sure as that of your cross-cultural worker. The responsible *action* you take is as important as the ministry your field worker performs.

And the *reward* of souls for His Kingdom will be equal to your missionary's and your own faithfulness.

A Case Study in Support

As a church in Sacramento, California began preparations to field their second missionary family, the concept of the church serving as senders became a priority. Seven couples committed themselves to direct the support team for Lou and Sandy and their six-month-old baby girl Marlies.

Each one on the team was encouraged to consider the seriousness of each support area. One of the team members tells the story:

Lou and Sandy invited nine couples to their home in June. They had already been to the Philippines. They had visited several ministries there— trusting that the Lord would show them where He wanted them to serve.

At the June meeting, Lou shared with us the opportunity they sensed God had provided for them. "But," he said, "the only way we will be able to go is if we have a Core Group responsible for our support." He discussed the basic needs for moral, logistics, financial, prayer, communication and re-entry support and how the Core Group would head up each of these areas. He then asked us to pray seriously about being a part of this team effort. He wanted our answer within two weeks. As it turned out, seven couples felt God's calling to serve. That was our beginning.

We all knew we wanted to support Lou and Sandy. After all, we had said we would be a part of the Core Group. But what was next? As Lou had asked George and me to head up the Core Group, we called the others to see if there was any specific area of ministry they would like to be involved in. The Hughes would head the logistics support. The Huffmans had a heart for re-entry. The Martins wanted to be responsible for communication support. Others responded in turn.

We had our first real meeting as a Core Group in August. At first I think we wanted to appear as if we had it "all together." As the meeting progressed, however, it became apparent that we, in fact, didn't! But praise God, the walls began to break down and we were able to admit that we were confused in some areas. As we began to discuss our problems, we also began to brainstorm as a group for answers.

So here's the opportunity for you to serve as a sender, to be a vital part of the mission process.

Hang on! As we'll see in the next chapter, there's more to it than raising your hand to volunteer. As your cross-cultural worker encounters difficulties, your *moral support* is needed to protect him.

(In addition to the following individual study, see the **Group Leader's Guide** for session one beginning on page 184.)

For Your Personal Involvement

Note: A text without a context is a pretext. Throughout this study you will find many Scripture references. To benefit more fully from the lessons, read each one in its full context. Allow the Holy Spirit to "guide you into all Truth" (John 16:13).

❑   Read Romans 10:13-15. From that passage fill in the blanks in the following statement. Notice that there is a key word in each question that leads you to the next question. The foundation of the whole sequence, then, lies in the final word!

10:13   For whosoever shall _____ upon the Name of the Lord shall be saved. (See Joel 2:32.)

10:14   How then shall they _____ on Him in Whom they have not _____? And how shall they _____ in Him of Whom they have not _____? And how shall they ____ without a _____?

10:15   And how shall they _____ except they are ____? (Write that final word in all capital letters to highlight in your mind the vitality of serving as senders!)

❑   List the nine stages of the physical/emotional/ psychological/spiritual life time-line of a missionary, and the incident in time that forms the transition from one to another. (Note the example.)

Period A: "Normal Living" ____; personal call
Period B:_____; _____
Period C:_____; _____
Period D:_____; _____
Period E:_____; _____

Period F:_____;_____
Period G:_____;_____
Period H:_____; <u>active in ministry</u>
Period I:_____

❑ Read the following passages relating to Paul's need for a support team. Place in each blank the type of support Paul was either asking for or expressing thanks for—whether moral, logistics, financial, prayer, communication or re-entry. (Each area is referred to in at least one passage.)

• Ephesians 6:18-19 _____
• 2 Timothy 4:13 _____
• Acts 14:26-28 _____
• Acts 21:12-13 _____
• Romans 16 _____
• Philippians 4:10-12 _____

❑ Indicate on the following pedestals where you think "cultural Christianity" estimates the value of:
• Pastor
• Lay person
• Missionary
• Evangelist

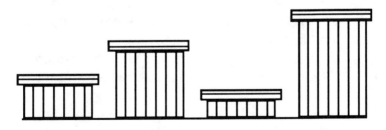

Did you put the lay person on the lowest stand?

Now read 1 Corinthians 1:11-13; 3:4-9; 12:12-27 and Revelation 2:6,15. The doctrine of the Nicolaitans made a distinction between the clergy (professional religious people) and the laity (common, ordinary folk).

After prayer, fill in the following sentence:

I, _____, as a sender,
         your name
am as important in God's global plan (but not more

important) as_____, even
         name a famous missionary
though my role won't seem as dramatic.

Maybe you can't fill that in right now. Go ahead and read through *Serving As Senders*. By the end of our study, we trust you *will* be able to make that statement personal!

Action Steps
By the time you have read Chapter One, completed the *For Your Personal Involvement* section and participated in a group discussion (See **Group Leader's Guide** beginning on page 184.), you should...
- Sense the need for those who serve as senders.
- Want to study further to know where you might fit in.
- Take the initiative. Let your missionary friend know that you are learning about the ministry of serving as a sender. And you will soon be available to help support him in one or more areas for God's glory!

• Multiply yourself. Look among your fellowship for those who seem to be at loose ends. Possibly they are the cross-cultural parts of your church. Invite them to read and study this book with you.

Chapter Two   Moral Support

"Be strong and very courageous; don't be afraid or dismayed: for the Lord your God is with you wherever you go."

Joshua 1:9

"It was a bit unusual. The rapid sequence of events, that is. We raised up others to assume our ministries in the church, got married, attended a 12-week field training course in Tijuana, Mexico, and spent our first year together living on a kibbutz in Israel!

"But why not? We were young, adventurous and had not yet accumulated a lot of the world's possessions. And most of all, the church where we had been ministering for the past three years was totally supportive. It was a small fellowship in a small town, so everyone knew us. The smiles and hugs on Sunday morning said to us, 'Scott and Jean, this is right!' Deep in our own hearts, God's peace said, 'This is right!'

"Invitations to our wedding included a note requesting, 'No gifts, please; we are going to Israel!' 'This is right!' they said with their donations of money instead. A prayer of blessing by our pastor at the wedding said, 'This is right!' Even our non-Christian parents said, 'This is right!' The moral support from every quarter said, 'This is right!'

"We began our training in Tijuana. We met our Mexican host family. Classes began. Learning how to relate

to each other—we had been married just four weeks—
was the subject of one of the classes. We did our field
work in the community: grappling with cultural adaptation, relating to our host family with our limited Span-
ish. But with their patience and a lot of humor, we
learned how to learn a second language and we bonded
with them. Principles of spiritual warfare were preparing
us for battle. We were learning how to live and minister
in a second culture. Communication from our home
church assured us that the sense of God's direction was
solid. 'This is right,' we said to each other.

"Then, as a part of our training to make sure the
support system was 'up and running,' we were sent
home for a long weekend. We sat in the pastor's living
room. Somehow there was an awkwardness. We glanced
at each other: 'This is not right!' we thought.

"Then Pastor Joe spoke: 'Scott and Jean, I have
made the decision that you are not to continue in this
mission!'

"We were stunned.

"Our objections were not too well thought-out and
they probably didn't make much sense since we were so
confused. My wife started crying. Pastor Joe said firmly,
'Jean, I am not moved by your tears!' We were speech-
less! We became angry but he remained firm: 'You are
not to go! If you continue, you are on your own!'

"We were dazed. The bottom had just fallen out! The
whole basis of our support team was shattered! There
was a very empty feeling in the pit of our stomachs. We
could hardly go to church. We weren't allowed to contact any of the people there for further support. 'This is
not right!' we knew.

"Fortunately, a part of our support team was made
up of individuals from several other churches and Bible
study groups. As we all beseeched the Lord for His direction in this new situation, we came to believe that it

wasn't that we shouldn't go, but that we were loosing a vital part of our support team.

"Just before leaving for Israel, by chance we met Pastor Joe downtown. He was so convinced that God had spoken to him that he said if we continued on this venture, something bad was going to happen to us in Israel. He would stake his ministry on it!

"Needless to say, this added insult to injury. Not only had we lost a strong foundation of moral support, but now this prediction was to cause a continual cloud of apprehension during our whole trip. When anything risky or unknown loomed ahead, we would remember his statement. For example, one night at the kibbutz, we were awakened by a loud siren. We were ready to run for the bomb shelter as we had often practiced. 'This is it! What bad thing is going to happen to us?' we thought. But since we saw no one else running and the siren stopped, we went back to bed.

"The next day we discovered that the temperature in the turkey house had fallen below a safe level. This siren was to alert the men responsible to adjust the thermostat! Though the humor of that situation mellowed our apprehension, Pastor Joe's 'cloud of doom' hovered above every crisis.

"We have returned home. It was a successful time of ministry in Israel. We're finding that God is slowly healing our relationships with the people of that church. Pastor Joe did not quit his ministry—in fact, he recently agreed for us to share in one of the local outreaches of his church!"

Moral support is the very foundation of the support system. Everyone in the church can be involved in this part of the ministry since in its most basic concept, moral support is simply saying, "God bless you! We are excited with you in your missionary venture!"

Did the great men and women of the Bible need moral support? Let's look at a few of them.

But David Encouraged Himself in the Lord

Jesse's other seven sons had been rejected. "For the Lord sees not as man sees; for man looks on the outward appearance, but the Lord looks on the heart." There yet remained one—a boy. A teenager. They brought him in from the fields where he was tending the sheep. And the Lord said, "Arise, anoint him, for this is he." And the Spirit of the Lord was on David from that day forward.

Through the battle with Goliath, through the struggle with Saul's insane jealousy, through the war of nerves during the months and years of fleeing and being pursued by a king who was troubled by an evil spirit, through the conflict involved in building his royal entourage of six hundred ruthless men, the Spirit of the Lord was upon David.

And as the Philistines were assembled against Israel, David and his men were with them. But a distrust of these Hebrews troubled the minds of the Philistines. David and his men were sent back to Ziklag—only to discover that the Amalekites had invaded from the south, burned the city and carried away all their wives and children. "And they wept, until they had no more power to weep. And David was deeply distressed, for the people spoke of stoning him. But David encouraged himself in the Lord" (see 1 Samuel 30).

Imagine the intensity of the moment—the physical distress of a three-day return march to Ziklag. The adrenaline flow building up to a battle against Israel and then the letdown. The bombarding emotions of losing family and possessions. The internal battle of "Lord, I am your anointed King of Israel. When am I going to possess the throne?" Where was David's moral support team? They wanted to stone him!

But David encouraged himself in the Lord.

My Hour Has Now Come

Eleven hundred years later. Another Man, another occasion. He says to His three-man support team, "My hour has come! My soul is exceedingly sorrowful and very heavy. Watch and pray with Me. And now the God-man, the Propitiation for our sins, the Lamb slain from before the foundations of the earth enters the most significant arena of battle of all time.

The battle of wills rages. All of His humanness rises to say, "Father, there must be another way. I cannot drink this cup of separation. We have been eternally One. Isn't there another way to redeem Man back to You? Let this cup pass from Me!"

The anguish becomes intense, for He knows there is no other way. The mental and spiritual suffering of the incarnate God in atonement for the sins of fallen man leads Him to the extreme of physical torture: hematidrosis, the bloody sweat.

"Could you not watch with Me one hour?" Jesus questioned His followers. Twice and then a third time, He came to them: "My hour has now come!"

In each of these situations there were those who could have been supportive. But David's men, so overcome by their own loss of wives and children and homes, thought only to stone David. Christ's men, self-indulgent in sleep, were not even aware of their Master's passion that night.

What of the others? When Mary told Joseph she was pregnant by the Holy Spirit, his first response was to put her away privately. In the Acts account of Peter's healing of the lame man, when the Jewish elders wanted the parents' testimony in support of their son's healing, in fear they said, "Ask him! He's old enough to tell you!" When Paul was determined to go to Jerusalem, throngs of people at two different times tried to dissuade him—even insisting that the Holy Spirit had instructed them to warn him.

The pages of history do not paint a brighter picture. Through the centuries, the pattern has not changed. Read about the bold men and women God told to go to the nations in Ruth Tucker's biographical history of Christian missions, *From Jerusalem to Irian Jaya* (see "Resources," page 199). You can count on the fingers of one hand the few who found strong moral support for their pioneer vision.

An English cobbler named William Carey struggled in the 1790s with the Church's responsibility to the Great Commission. Later he was to become known as the "Father of Modern Missions." But in his early days as the vision stirred deep in his heart, there was no support. His fellow churchmen openly rebuked him by saying, "When God pleases to convert the heathen, He will do it without your aid or ours." His wife initially refused to join him on his voyage to India. Only a delay in the departure date gave her the opportunity to reconsider.

Today as thousands of cross-cultural workers emerge from their closets of prayer, having grappled with the issues of being His soldiers of the cross in another culture, what sort of moral support can they anticipate from people?

• People so lost in their narrow world that they do not support God's anointed but rather begin hurling stones of incrimination—like David's men?

• People lulled into self-indulgent sleep to the extent that they are unaware of God's plan for their friends—like Christ's men?

• People so concerned about public opinion that they want to nod nicely at missionary zeal but try to send you away privately—like Joseph?

• People so afraid for the other programs of their church that they don't want anything to do with daring adventures into the unknown, the uncomfortable? Mission ministry, after all, could be regarded as competition to the status quo—according to non-moral-supporters like the Jewish elders.

• People so sure that they have "heard from the Lord" that your "hearing from the Lord" is wrong—like Paul's friends?

• People who pierce God's missionary heart by distorting their theology—like Carey's friends?

Stones That Do Not Support

Stones of incrimination. There are few who can handle the personal challenge presented to them by a friend who thinks God wants him to do such a bold, daring thing as go to the mission field. Whether ignorantly, out of well-meaning friendship or to assuage their own feelings of distress, they may begin hurling stones of recrimination: "Man, it's a rough world out there! Riots and wars! Hatred and violence! You could get yourself killed!"

Other callous responses might be: "You've got to be kidding! You? A missionary? What do you think you can do to save the world?"

Often close, loving friends counsel:

• You're needed here. You have so much to offer right here in our fellowship.

• Waste your education out in the middle of nowhere? What will your dad say? After all, he paid the bill for your college degree!

• Why don't you get a real job? Go make some money so you'll be secure; later on you can think about getting involved in missions.

• You can't offend your mother that way! How can you take her grandkids away from her? They need her!

• What about your kids' education? They will come home ignoramuses and social misfits!

• You expect to get married out there? You'll never meet anybody!

In a final lament, abandoning all logic, they may cry, "I don't believe this is happening to me!"

The cross-cultural worker who has already battled it out with the Lord over feelings of inadequacy sits in a disheveled heap—beneath a pile of stones, battered and hurting. The few and the strong who make it encourage themselves in the Lord. But it would be so much better if they had you as a part of their Moral Support Team to encourage them.

Self-indulgent sleep is the state of too large a segment of today's Church. Self-indulgence has produced a myopic introspection; we seem to focus on healing ourselves so we can have nicer lives. "Lord, comfort me so I will be comfortable" is in direct contrast to what is told the church in 2 Corinthians 1:4.

We want to be comfortable and we want security. We feel uneasy about unpredictability—like Peter as he blurted in his threatened loss of security, "Lord, I won't let You die!" (Matthew 16:22).

Our society's drive for the "Great American Dream" has become a nightmare! It keeps many potential moral supporters lulled in a stupor of inactivity.

Perhaps the "Barnabas and Saul" of your fellowship come back from an Urbana Student Mission Conference, a two-week mini-mission or a summer of service sensing the greatness of God's plan of the ages and their privileged part in it. Perhaps in your church, as in too many others, few barely rouse themselves to hear these enthusiasts report on what God is doing globally. As the church nods off, the potential missionaries say, "Could you not listen to what I believe God has in store for us for just one minute?"

The cross-cultural worker goes back to the Rock and prays again, "Father, there must be some other way for You to accomplish Your purpose than by having me go."

"No, My child. This is the way. Walk ye in it." And his hour comes. No support is given. All scatter. And the cross-cultural worker faces the Judases and priests and mobs of this world on his own—unless you are there to give him your moral support.

Worries about public opinion can hurt a missionary. Perhaps the potential cross-cultural worker is told, "Okay, if you have to go, go. But don't rock the boat. Don't get the people here involved—especially financially. What will happen to our other programs?"

Fortunately, it is getting harder and harder for churches to have this attitude because mission organizations and those agencies helping to prepare cross-cultural workers for service are insisting that the local fellowship take the initiative in the missions process.

However, tragically, there are still thousands of cases in which a mission candidate's pastor is the "last to know." Or perhaps he never finds out! Public opinion in some churches does not allow for radical moves into international evangelization. So the cross-cultural worker has to leave very quietly—unless you are there to shout an encouraging, "Bon voyage!"

Other attitudes dry up your cross-cultural worker's supply of moral support.

Competition within the Body of Christ scares some fellowships into undermining a mission candidate's moral support. The message might be very strong: "We don't want to lose you."

It wasn't that the Jews did not believe in world evangelization. For Christ said of them, "You travel over land

and sea to make one convert" (Matthew 23:15). Nor was it that they were against His healing people. But throngs of people were following Jesus. He was a threat to the establishment. He was the competition. He didn't fit into their programs.

The bold, the daring, the aggressive plans of the world missionary community don't fit into the programs of a lot of today's churches, either—unless you are there to encourage Christ's example of unity in diversity.

Contradictory counsel can discourage a missionary. The Apostle Paul sensed at every turn the potential of the enemy's move. "I will stay in Ephesus until Pentecost, for God has opened a great and effectual door, and with many adversaries" (1 Corinthians 16:8-9). At Miletus he wrote, "I am compelled by the Spirit to go to Jerusalem. I don't know what may happen to me there, except that the Holy Spirit warns me that imprisonment and persecution await me in every city that I visit" (Acts 20:22-23).

So when his disciples said to Paul "through the Holy Spirit" that he should not go up to Jerusalem, he had to defend his certainty of God's direction. Instead of receiving support, he had to rebuke his friends: "What do you mean by unnerving me with all your tears. You are breaking my heart! I am not only ready to be bound, but to die for the sake of the name of the Lord Jesus."

Luke wrote, "And when we could not dissuade [Paul], we held our tongues and said, 'The Lord's will be done!'" (Acts 21:13-14). They gave him the silent treatment. The raised eyebrows. The shrugged shoulders. The anxious, "Just wait—you'll see."

And the one who is boldly doing the work of the Lord is left alone—unless you are there to provide moral support to sustain your missionary in his difficult times when the adversaries are opposing him.

Distorted theological views can end up damaging the morale of a cross-cultural worker. The missionary heart of God is pierced again and again as fellowships deny the biblical injunctions to go preach and teach.

Some shout it as brashly as did William Carey's contemporaries: "God will do it without us if He wants it done!" Others say it more subtly: "We're too young as a fellowship. We're not big enough yet. No one in our fellowship seems interested. We don't have the resources to support a missionary. I don't have the time to devote to another new project. We would only want to send our best, and we can't afford to lose our leadership."

Those excuses and a thousand more have all been thought or spoken. Yet not a one of them stands the test of exposure to Scripture. Each excuse shrinks into the shadows, trying to hide from the Light of His Word. There is no theology to deny the missionary heartbeat of our God Who is "not willing that any perish, but that all come to repentance!" (2 Peter 3:9).

Therefore, the cross-cultural parts of the Body—and there are cross-cultural parts, or else it is not a Body— hang lifeless in atrophy for lack of exercise. Or if they are challenged by another church or agency, their home church is jealous because they are drawn away. And we are all the losers for it.

The story is told of a young sailor who was making final preparations for a solo voyage around the world in his homemade craft. Throngs of people crowded the small mooring as he stowed the last boxes of provisions. A murmuring air of pessimistic concern exploded into a volume of discouragement: "Son, you'll never make it! That boat will not withstand the waves of the storms! You'll run out of food! The sun will broil you!"

A late arriver, hearing all of these discouraging warnings, felt an irresistible desire to offer some optimism and encouragement. As the little craft began sailing away from the pier, he pushed his way to the end of the dock. Waving his hands wildly, he kept shouting, "*Bon voyage!* You're really somebody! We're with you! We're proud of you! God be with you, brother!"

The world seems to offer two kinds of support: "Wait 'til you get out in that cold, cruel world. It's rough!" And those who exude a contagious, confident *"Bon voyage!"*

There are dozens of thoughtless ways to burst the balloon of your aspiring missionary. But there are also plenty of ways you can buoy up his enthusiasm with solid moral support.

Some Holy Spirit-guided soul-searching of our own attitudes toward cross-cultural ministry would be good at this point. An initial clearing of these stones of incrimination will make way for another type of stone—the foundation for building a strong support system for the cross-cultural outreach ministry of your church.

How to Give Solid-As-A-Rock Moral Support
Dan had heard the call of God on his life to go. He had visited Thailand on several occasions. There he had seen the hunger of pastors to learn how to study the Word. He had experienced the joy of helping them satisfy that hunger through the seminars he taught.

And now Dan was sure God was directing him to a longer-term commitment: to establish a ministry of conducting seminars for national pastors of Asia, seminars designed to train pastors in the study of the Word, thus allowing them to better feed their flocks.

But Dan was the pastor of a church in the United States. It would not be easy to leave the people. He had founded the church. Who would fill his position? How could he uproot his family and move them into the unknown? What about the finances and logistics of that move? What about communication and prayer? Where would they stay when they came home?

All of these questions and apprehensions were real and needed answers. But they were more easily handled because the entire congregation gave their full moral support to what they sensed from the Lord to be a "new thing" for Dan and for them!

Moral support is the foundation of the sending process. Moral support is the *"Bon voyage"* of those who serve as senders to those who go. Moral support is as much an attitude that your cross-cultural worker will sense as it is an action you can do.

Let's look at some solid foundation stones.

Jesus is the Chief Cornerstone

There first, of course, has to be a cornerstone, "...a tried stone, a precious cornerstone, a sure foundation" (Isaiah 28:16). In Jesus' day, the cornerstone was not some memorial plaque mortared into the wall after the building was completed. It was the first stone set. All measurements of height, length and breadth were taken from it. If it were well-placed, the building had a good chance of being well-constructed. But if it were poorly laid, watch out!

Christ's life and teachings were an example of moral support. In fact, when Matthew wrote his Gospel, the Holy Spirit inspired him to recall how Jesus fulfilled Isaiah's prophecy: "The bruised reed shall He not break, and the smoking (dimly burning) flax shall He not quench" (Matthew 12:20 quoting Isaiah 42:3). A more current rendering is, "He does not crush the weak, nor snuff out the smallest candle flame." "He doesn't kick you when you're down!" might be an appropriate paraphrase.

What *does* He do?

He takes the bruised reed by the hand and, lifting her up, says, "Where are your accusers? Has no one condemned you? Neither do I condemn you. Go and sin no more!" (John 8:1-11). He meets the "smoking flax" at night since Nicodemus feared the Jews; He gently breathes the Spirit of Life into the failing embers (John 3:1-21). Peter's tears of remorse had all but extinguished his flame of fire. Jesus tenderly fans those failing embers back to life with His trilogy of poignant questions: "Peter, do you love Me? Feed My sheep!" (John 21:15-18).

His example of refusing to condemn and determining to encourage is the cornerstone of our support structure as we serve as senders. But it's not enough just to do His deeds. No amount of human-level determination will equip you to be an adequate sender if you're not an intimate disciple of Jesus Christ. This topic is beyond our focus of study, but every sender, every sending team must be personally, constantly communing with the One Who in moral support told us, "As My Father has sent Me, even so send I you" (John 20:21). *The Jesus Style,* a book by Gayle D. Erwin gives valuable and practical instruction on this subject (see "Resources," page 199).

The Simplicity of Moral Support

The cornerstone has been laid. We can begin building. The first foundation stone that nudges right up and fits so perfectly beside the Chief Cornerstone is the moral support of the church that helps cross-cultural workers to "Do it simply—and simply do it!"

Jesus was a master at reducing to simplicity the impassioned issues of His day—and ours.

On the complex issue of taxation, He said, "Whose image is on the coin?"

"Caesar's," was the answer.

"Well, you had better give it to him then. But also give to God what belongs to Him!"

We spend hours questioning what life is all about.

Where did we come from? Jesus simply said, "I came from the Father." We spend days wondering why we're here. Jesus said, "I am doing the will of the Father." We spend years worrying where we're going. Jesus said, "I am going to the Father." In simple yet precise terms, He answered the three universal questions of life! (See John 13:1-15.)

Jesus' ministry was deep, yet simple. And His lifestyle was also simple. He was born in a stable. He had no place to call home. His body occupied a borrowed tomb at His death.

As your cross-cultural worker begins taking the steps toward the fields of the world, a thousand opportunities and ways to minister will begin bombarding him. Encourage him to keep his eyes focused on the simple, straightforward ministry of Jesus. Urge him to listen quietly to the direction of the Spirit out of all the godly counsel he is receiving. (See Proverbs 19:20-21.) Remind him to keep it simple; he's not some new messiah! Advise him also to simply do it—to keep going one step at a time.

Help him practice a "wartime lifestyle" even before going to the field. This doesn't mean living under an austere, ascetic vow of poverty. It means trimming off what isn't necessary. It means not spending on some things and spending strategically on others—much as a soldier going into combat doesn't need a gold-embossed jogging suit but does need a very expensive, state-of-the-art rifle.

Encouraging simplicity in ministry goals and in lifestyle is moral support!

Integrating Missions

The next foundation stone also fits snugly in its place. Support your worker in his perspective that mission is an *integrated* ministry of the church. Cross-cultural outreach is not the only God-ordained ministry.

"Yes, it is exciting to see that God has chosen you to minister cross-culturally. Yes, the zeal of the Lord is upon you," you can agree with your missionary friend. But then you must remind him that the Sunday school teachers who tolerated his elementary distractions are now dealing with the next generation of field workers. Therefore, their work continues to be vital.

All the parts of the Body work together in one direction within the "unchangeable purpose of God" (see Hebrews 6:11-18), each adding its own expertise. Some of these ministries are more direct in that ultimate purpose of the Church—to bless with the Good News every people, tribe and tongue. And some are indirectly related.

You can encourage your missionary to remember that an accurate, big-picture worldview integrates ministries; it doesn't eliminate some nor value one ministry above another.

God's great purpose incorporates every God-given discipline in your life, every ministry in the life of your church. For example:

When your church's shut-in visitation team ministers to the elderly by sharing songs and holding hands and listening to reminiscences, they can bring specific prayer requests of the urgent needs of all the ministries of the church. They can school the elderly in how to pray against the strongholds of Satan over a particular people group your missionary is targeting. They can infuse into each shut-in's remaining days the magic elixir of purpose—"You can spend time in prayer that we can't! You know more about life than we do, therefore you can pray specifically for the ups and downs of our mission team. You can help break open the way for the Gospel in this group as you pray against the principalities and powers that rule and blind them! We need you!"

A church shut-in ministry can be incorporated into the vision of Christ's global cause, whether they pray for your missionary or for the church's prison ministry.

Every God-ordained ministry of the church can be expanded as it aligns its purposes with the great, unchangeable purpose of God. The life of the whole Body—not just the cross-cultural parts—must remain strong. Therefore, the worship leaders must continue to usher us into the very throne room of God, and the teachers of the Word must continue to feed the flock. And the other outreach ministries of the church must continue to reach out.

This is not easy for a missionary to appreciate as he gets into his ministry. His part of the big picture of God's purpose can easily become the only activity he sees. Therefore, you enter as his moral supporter to give him a godly perspective.

You are able to help him recognize that moral support is a two-way street: To enjoy the moral support of others demands that he be interested in and an encouragement to them in their endeavors.

Active Listening

Another foundation stone of moral support is the art of active listening. Paul Tournier in his book *To Understand Each Other* said, "Most conversations of this world are 'dialogues of the deaf.'" Emotional isolation is already a major problem in North America. So when your friend is grappling with all the uncertainties of moving into cross-cultural outreach ministry, he needs even greater support: he needs your listening ear.

When your friend shares his thoughts about cross-cultural involvement, your ministry of moral support is most effective as you simply sit and listen.

Active listening is probably one of the most neglected foundation stones of moral support. *Active listening* says, "I am with you. I will take the time. I will put energy into really listening to your heart, not just to what your surface words are saying."

Active listening calls for all of your attention. It is hard work; it requires concentration. But how necessary it is to moral support!

Active listening obligates you to respond with respect. Even though you are not "in his shoes" and cannot fully comprehend what he is experiencing, you can express empathy. Try to sense his thoughts and feelings as he anticipates his venture of faith.

Active listening demands that you give feedback. Repeat in your own words what you heard him say. For example, imagine yourself listening to Scott and Jean after their traumatic meeting with Pastor Joe as recounted at the beginning of this chapter:

Scott says, "Then Pastor Joe spoke and said, 'I have made the decision that you are not to continue in this mission!' Man, we were stunned!"

You say, "I guess so!"

"No kidding," says Jean. "I guess our objections were not too well thought-out."

You say, "You mean your objections to his objections?"

Jean laughs. "Yeah, I guess so. What we said probably didn't make much sense since we were so confused."

You say, "Your thoughts were too scattered to explain to him how you knew God wants you to go."

"Right," says Scott. "We sure know how to explain it to people now after that experience!"

"Feels good to be confident about God's direction, doesn't it?"

"It sure does—even in spite of Pastor Joe's response...."

And you've effectively listened through a painful experience that needed to be shared. Further, you've also allowed Scott and Jean to work through some of their feelings about the incident until they begin to have some positive feelings about it. Your active listening and repeating what you thought you heard have resulted in a great show of solid moral support!

Just being there to listen with positive feedback helps your missionary clarify his thoughts and feelings on a host of new concepts he must process.

We all know the risks of international travel. We all know the dangers of terrorist activity. We all know the socio-political issues concerning the rise in nationalism. We all know the fears of the unknown. God does, too. Yet He says go!

Will you be one of those who will say, "Wow! What a privilege to be about our Father's business!"? Will you offer, "We're with you! What can we do to help?" You can be one who shouts, "God bless you! We're proud of you! You're really something! *Bon voyage!*"

Stone by stone, the foundation of moral support is being laid.

Commissioning as Moral Support

There may be other stones of solid moral support that His Spirit will bring to your mind. But for now let's consider just three more stones that are vital to this foundation: called, counseled and commissioned. The church in Antioch provides a model from which we can draw our examples.

They put five men forward; they fasted and prayed. They heard the Holy Spirit say, "We want Barnabas and Saul." They fasted and prayed some more; they laid their hands on them. They sent them away. Who is "they"? The church, the local Body of believers—those who were sharing their own concern for this ministry that was burning deep in the hearts of Barnabas and Saul (see Acts 13).

Called.

The church, the home fellowship, the missions fellowship, the prayer group, the college and career class—some group besides the ones wanting to go need to hear the Holy Spirit say, "Separate unto Me [the Barnabas and Saul from your fellowship] for the task to which I have called them." This confirmation provides tremendous moral support! It is one thing for your missionary to think the Lord has directed him. It is incredibly more reassuring to know He has confirmed it in the hearts of others as well.

Counseled.

The church fasted and prayed some more (Acts 13:3). Though Scripture isn't specific as to their prayers, it's apparent they were seeking guidance from the Lord for details of this new venture. The passage implies that a group larger than the two going heard answers to these questions: How should they go? Where is the money coming from? What do they take with them? When should they go? What are they going to do when they get there? Where is *there*? (See Matthew 10:1-16.)

This was a first as this team of senders determined how they could best be supportive to some of the Church's first missionaries. Remember, the Antioch church was filled with ordinary human beings. Yet they were able to carry the weight of these unprecedented decisions as a team of people who had, in fasting and prayer, heard the Lord's direction.

Commissioned.

The senders laid their hands on the missionaries (Acts 13:3).

In Hebrews 6, the laying on of hands is named as one of the foundational doctrines. In this situation, the event was a commissioning, a setting-apart for a specific task, an identifying with the upcoming ministry of the sent ones.

Whether your cross-cultural worker is going short-term or longer, he needs the spiritual covering—the moral support—of "the laying on of hands," because, as an extension of your church's ministry, he is going out to battle against the enemy.

Identifying with your missionary, of course, means that you'll need to do some fine-tuning of your understanding of what he'll be facing. You need to know what God is doing these days in cross-cultural outreach ministry. Become an expert on the steady progress of the 21st century's Great Commission endeavor.

Read how Jackie Pullinger broke through the Walled City of Hong Kong in *Chasing the Dragon*. Marvel at how a 19-year-old touched the lives of Latin American Indians in *Bruchko* by Bruce Olson. Weep in sorrow at the price Christ paid for the lost of Russia as you read *Vanya* by Myrna Grant or *Tortured For His Faith* by Haralan Popov. Understand the cost of commitment in Pakistani Muslim Bilquis Sheikh's *I Dared to Call Him Father*. *Anointed for Burial* recounts God's work in Cambodia just before its fall. F. Kefa Sempangi gives a first person account of the martyrdom of Christians in Uganda in *A Distant Grief*. Rejoice that God has placed *Eternity in Their Hearts* as examined in Don Richardson's book on redemptive analogy, a key to proclaiming Christ to the nations. (See "Resources," beginning on page 199 for information on obtaining these and other cutting-edge materials on today's mission to the world.)

As you identify with your missionary's work, what you learn about God's work around the world will bring a deeper sense of your part in God's global purpose and of how your role is critical as you give moral support to those who say, "I believe the Lord wants me to go to the mission field! And I want you, church, to send me!"

A Case Study in Moral Support

More members of the sending team we met in Chapter One recount some of their experiences in learning how to offer their missionaries some solid moral support:

Those of us who know Lou and Sandy personally would probably sum up our offers of moral support to them in these words: "We love you and are here to help you in any way we can. We believe in the vision the Lord has given you to go to the Philippines. But in our eagerness to help you on your way, don't lose sight of the fact that we will dearly miss you."

After the Core Group—which is what we call the leadership of our Lou-and-Sandy support team— was established in June, things began to roll at seemingly breakneck speed. Looking back on it all now, we see that the moral support we gave was intertwined with our actions in all the other areas of support. When Lou and Sandy had to get out of their duplex and into temporary lodging for one month before leaving for training in Mexico, a home was graciously opened to them.

Have you ever prepared for a garage sale? Lou and Sandy had to go through every single material possession they owned: Do we sell this? Store it? Take it with us? Ultimately the decisions were Lou and Sandy's, but to be nearby with a listening ear and an opinion was part of our moral support. The willingness of people to find boxes, store things safely, build a crate for shipment, advertise the sale, price everything and bring over the meals again and again after the pots and pans were packed expressed the moral support so needed and appreciated by Lou and Sandy.

Since they have left, we have found other ways to give moral support. Their last Sunday at church we had a large banner made which said, "*Bon voyage,*

Lou, Sandy and Marlies." We later laid it out over several long tables and provided pens for people to write some words of encouragement. We shipped the banner by boat so they would receive it after having been there for several months.

About six weeks after they left, baby Marlies had her first birthday. At our next Core Group meeting we had balloons, party hats, cake and ice cream and kids. We sang "Happy Birthday" to the absent guest of honor. We videotaped the fun. Because we had time left on the tape, we brought the camcorder to church Sunday and had friends give Lou, Sandy and Marlies a special hello.

The enthusiasm and excitement that still accompanies any of the activities we do for our missionaries lets us know the moral support is running high. Though letter writing generally falls into the category of communication support, the fact that Lou and Sandy receive so many letters is most certainly a boost to their morale. In one six-week period, they reported they had gone only three days without receiving at least one letter, and one day they had received seven!

Moral support is obviously basic if you're serving as a sender. Maybe your forte as a sender will be boosting your missionary's morale.

But other phases of support are important, too, if your sent-one is going to be fully supported. Somebody has to help with the nuts and bolts of stretching your fellowship's ministry from Jerusalem to Judea to Samaria and to the uttermost parts of the earth! Missionaries need careful, solid logistics support.

(In addition to the individual study below, see the **Group Leader's Guide** for session two beginning on page 186.)

For Your Personal Involvement
• Read Matthew 12:20 from a number of translations. Choose one that really communicates the message to you. Memorize it. Meditate on it. Allow the Holy Spirit to infuse this concept of moral support into the very fiber of your being.
• Read, in its context, the story of each of the individuals in the Bible we referred to. Place next to their names the relationship of the people who could have been of moral support to them:

David, 1 Samuel 30 _____

Jesus, Luke 22 _____

Mary, Matthew 1 _____

The blind man, John 9 _____

Paul, Acts 21 _____

• Choose one of the stories. In your own words, retell the story as if those people *had* given moral support.
• Because moral support is a two-way street, it would be interesting to survey your Sunday school teachers with the question: "When our missionaries have been home for an extended time, have any of them ever thanked you for teaching our kids? Have you ever thanked them for representing us in cross-cultural ministry?" Share your survey results with your pastor.
• Name several commercial jingles that, if followed, could easily distract you from giving moral support to your missionaries. For example: "When the going gets tough, the tough go shopping."

What are some *biblical* proverbs to govern our actions in moral support?

Action Steps

By the time you have read Chapter Two, completed the *For Your Personal Involvement* section and participated in a discussion group, you should...

• Understand that moral support is the basic foundation of the support system.

• Express appreciation and give moral support to everyone in the fellowship who is a functioning part of the Body.

• Realize that moral support is an ongoing relationship with your missionary.

• Write to one of your missionaries on the field and say, "Here is my belated *'Bon voyage!'* God bless you!"

• Multiply yourself. You might be surprised how contagious enthusiastic moral support becomes! Encourage others with the practice of encouragement!

Chapter Three   Logistics Support

"And when you come, please bring the cloak I left with Carpus at Troas and the books, but especially the parchments."

2 Timothy 4:13

"Sure, I had had some good training in building a support team. I had made provision for my logistics support. A real neat guy named Bill had said he would handle everything. Looking back, that should have been my first clue that this might not work out. *Nobody* can handle everything! But I didn't think of it at the time.

"A ministry opportunity had opened up. We had been invited to lead a relief work in the Middle East. We sensed God's direction in this. Things were coming together well. A lot of clothes and medicine were being given to us to distribute once we got there. We neatly packed and identified each box. Bill said that when sailors from our church came to a nearby military installation, he would have them each carry a few. Or he was sure he could arrange space for the whole shipment through diplomatic channels. What a relief to my mind. I could concentrate on other details.

"Three years later, we came home for a short visit. I sheepishly went to the friend who had let us store those boxes in his garage, lo, these three years. Yep! They were all there! Just as we had left them! Not a one had been sent to us.

"We shipped the stuff to a ministry in Mexico. They said they could use what wasn't outdated. I took the few remaining boxes of our personal items to Bill. 'Yeah, sure! No problem. Those will be on the next ship out!'

"Well, we're ready to come home on furlough again. We've decided that since we've made it for six years over here without that stuff, we really don't need it. It will be interesting, though, when we get home to look through the boxes to see what one day had seemed so important to us.

"Bill's a good man. But he just didn't seem to be able to get those boxes over to us!"

Logistics Support deals with handling the nuts and bolts of your cross-cultural worker's continuing home country responsibilities.

Logistics support must be considered on two levels: 1) Those areas of business to be attended to by the church leadership or missionary agency, and 2) the multitude of details that can be handled by a team of individuals. You, as part of the Logistics Support Team, could find yourself involved in:

- Identifying the cross-cultural workers in your fellowship.
- Maintaining accountability in ministry.
- Confirming and encouraging spiritual growth.
- Managing business affairs.
- Attending to personal details.

Identifying Cross-Cultural Workers

The local congregation, the Body of Christ in micro-cosm, in order to function as a Body, must have all the necessary parts. The Body needs a mouth, so He appointed some prophets and pastor/teachers. The Body needs to function "decently and in order," so He gave some the gift of administration.

He even has someone always "just hanging around" like the appendix! And because *outreach* is one of the main functions of the Church, and because He said, "The field is the world" (Matthew 13:38), God has placed in every Body parts that are to minister cross-culturally.

In many churches, cross-cultural workers have not been given the opportunity to exercise their gifts, so they sit in atrophy, wondering, "Why am I here?" They may try to find a place of ministry in some other area, but they just don't fit in! So in frustration they move from one ministry to another—or from one church to another.

The first logistical responsibility of the church, then, is to provide for the identification and exercise of the cross-cultural parts.

When Barnabas and Saul returned to Antioch from Jerusalem with some firsthand reports from the Apostles, the church identified and put forth five men—prophets and teachers, leaders in the church. Then, in prayer and fasting, *the church* heard the Holy Spirit say, "I want Barnabas and Saul for some cross-cultural work" (A rather loose paraphrase of Acts 13:1-2!).

The local fellowship of believers must take the initiative in the missionary process by identifying the cross-cultural parts of the Body and allowing them to exercise their gifts.

A missions fellowship at your church , then, becomes an ideal testing ground for potential missionaries. Under the direction of a lay or staff leader, those who believe they are your Body's cross-cultural parts can experience all aspects of missions. They can be challenged to the task of cross-cultural outreach ministry by speakers and cultural studies and reports. They can practice the art of missionary support—moral, logistics and so on. They can exercise their gifts by ministering to the internationals in your own home town. As potential *goers* are identified, they can actually go on a mini-mission or short-term experience. And the identified *senders* can serve as their senders!

The pastor, missions committee or fellowship should not be the last to know when one of the members from your church is getting involved in missions! Take the initiative: Make cross-cultural outreach a part of the vision God has given you for your fellowship.

Maintaining Accountability In Ministry

Accountability has become one of the catchwords of our culture. And wouldn't one expect a reaction—at some time—to the "do your own thing" philosophy? Yet, from across the nation, there are hundreds of pastors and church leaders who do not know what those who have gone out from their church are doing. Some say, "Well, they're with XYZ Ministry. Isn't that a good mission?"

Quite possibly. But....

Is that mission an extension of the ministry goals of your church? Is that ministry targeting a decisive point of battle? Is your missionary's abilities and giftings suited to the work of that mission?

A second dimension of this responsibility then follows: Once you are sure your cross-cultural worker is involved in a ministry suited to his gifts and the ministry thrust of your church, you must have some ongoing evaluation to know if that ministry is progressing. A regular, independent report from his supervisor will keep you in touch with his work.

If your missionary is working through a mission agency, make sure the lines of accountability relationship are open, defined and include your fellowship. Remember, this missionary is still a part of your Body.

A report from your worker should fill in the details. A periodic phone call, an occasional report from another worker in the area—even a visit by an appointed elder from your church would assure you that the ministry is really happening.

After all, the work of those who go and those who serve as senders is a team effort!

Confirming Spiritual Growth
Sadly, some sets of statistics report that for all their preparation, for all their "hearing God's voice" and for all their support, up to 50% of cross-cultural workers do not complete their *first* term of commitment.

Too many of them don't make it because of spiritual drought. They have dried up spiritually. They have come to the point where they are trying to give out more than they are taking in.

Church leadership must encourage spiritual growth 1) before missionaries go, 2) while they're on the field and 3) when they return home.

1) Encouragement in spiritual growth before they go.
Antioch provides a good example: Barnabas and Saul were mature leaders chosen by the Holy Spirit for a very tough assignment. It is easy to study their fine qualifications in Scripture.

For some reason, however, they took John Mark along. Evidently he was not prepared; when the going got tough, he quit!

Several years later, Paul sensed that John Mark *still* was not ready (Acts 15:38). But then several years after that assessment, Paul told Timothy to bring Mark with him, for "he is profitable for the ministry" (2 Timothy 4:11).

A goer's eagerness to be sent doesn't necessarily mean he is *ready* to be sent.

One church does it this way: Everyone who even thinks he is a cross-cultural part of the Body is encouraged to attend the missions fellowship headed by a cross-cultural coordinator. Here they are regularly exposed to cross-cultural outreach through prayer for the peoples of the world, speakers and videos of ministries, opportunities for ministry and short-term awareness and ministry trips.

As a person (or couple) *and* the group sense the call of the potential goer, that person begins relating with the senior pastor in personal discipleship training. When he is raised to the position of deacon in the church and has functioned for a time in some place of leadership, he is ready for cultural training and developing a personal support team.

The church must send a capable, credible worker—one who knows what he believes and why. That confidence may come through in-house training, sending him to a Bible school or a combination of several preparation programs.

The church must send one who has stripped the Gospel and teachings of Christ of all American, Greek and Hebrew culture so that he can allow his host culture to clothe the Gospel in garb suitable to them.

Senders must send one who has been trained in

interpersonal relationships, the lack of which is the greatest reason for missionary dropouts! The church must not send one who is "ever learning, yet never able to come to the knowledge of the truth" (2 Timothy 3:7), but one who is "increasing in the knowledge of God" (Colossians 1:10).

2) Encouragement in spiritual growth on the field.

Once a field worker becomes unencumbered with the affairs of his life back home (see 2 Timothy 2:4) and is thrust into the midst of unending opportunity for ministry, it is *very easy* for him to neglect his own spiritual intake—to be working so hard for the Vine that the branch becomes pinched and the life-sustaining sap is cut off.

Soon yesterday's prayers, last week's Bible reading, last month's study in the Word are not able to sustain the worker through today's demands. And he falls prey to spiritual drought.

The writer of Hebrews says, "At a time when you should be feeding others, I am having to bottle-feed you.... Let's not lay over and over the foundation doctrines..., but let's go on to maturity" (Hebrews 5:12-6:3).

Because your worker doesn't have five Christian radio stations, two Christian TV stations and a dozen Bible studies to choose from each week, he must be a student of the Word—one who knows how to rightly divide the Word of Truth, a workman who doesn't need to be ashamed (2 Timothy 2:15). He must know how to feed himself spiritually.

You may help in this area by sending Bible study tapes to him, or by having him commit to a correspondence course. Perhaps you can study along with him by letter on a book by book Bible study.

One missionary family in Peru arranged for their church to send weekly Bible study tapes. They soon began to listen to them in a group Bible study with other team members. Before long many groups were organized and listening! When they heard a few new choruses on the study tapes, they began to miss their Christian music. They quickly got on the ham radio to ask a support team member to send some Christian music tapes down—soon!

3) Encouragement in spiritual growth when they come back home.

Your missionary may be home for a brief stay before he returns to the field. Check his spiritual temperature. Many have been bombarded by new ideas and ideals, different values and beliefs. Is he still anchored to the Rock? Are the changes in his thinking only cultural? Or has a subtle pantheism or another deceptive world system outlook permeated his doctrine? He may need a strengthening of his faith. More seriously, he may need a redefining of his Christian foundations. Some slightly askew winds of doctrine may have even come from the isolated team of the organization through which he is working.

If your worker has come home to take up a new ministry here, you cannot presume that his spiritual growth will continue. Here at home he is bombarded by the gods of materialism and hedonism. These can have a drastic effect on his doctrine! Make sure he is still sharing what he "first received from the Lord" (1 Corinthians 15:3).

A certain family served on a two-year mission venture in the Orient. They returned to the States to resume ministry. It wasn't until much later—fifteen years later—through the counsel of their church leadership, that they came to understand the intensity of a spiritual assault that had been launched against their whole family while overseas. They then began to work on breaking the powers of darkness and the resulting destructive patterns and began to live in the victorious freedom available in Christ. Supportive, intense prayer for them by the Body when they first came home might have identified this problem sooner.

Managing Business Affairs

If your worker goes through a mission agency, most of the following issues will be established by the agency's policy. Reading through some of these perplexing logistics might make you appreciate what an agency goes through to keep your missionary on the field. Even if these tasks are handled by an agency, it is still your responsibility to know the agency's policies and how you as the sending church relate to them. More and more mission agencies are asking for the church to be more actively involved in the whole missions process—including logistics.

If your church sends out missionaries directly to work with national ministries or to plant churches in unreached groups, think and plan very seriously through each of the following issues first. And remember that the list is only a cursory look at the business matters that will come up!

1) Money

This one word conjures up more emotion than any other in the whole arena of missions! Because of its importance, someone in the church leadership must be responsible to handle its details:

a) Work with the national ministry and your cross-cultural worker to determine a necessary and adequate monthly budget.

b) Establish acceptable methods for securing enough financing.

c) Communicate how each donor identifies his gift as designated for a particular missionary and/or project.

d) Develop a system for receipting the donor and notifying your cross-cultural worker of amounts and who donated. Careful financial monitoring is needed to actually transfer those funds to the field. Will any be kept back for administering the funding process? What will you do if donations fall below the established quota?

2) Taxes

How easily Jesus reduced to simplicity the whole issue of taxes (see Matthew 33:15-22). But earthly governments seem to be able to make things very complicated. Therefore "rendering unto Caesar" requires an astute mind knowledgeable of the myriads of details involved. Details such as deductions, tax status changes caused by your worker's ordination and length of residency outside the US and the host country's taxation just begin to open this Pandora's Box!

And, remember, tax laws are in a continual state of change. If your fellowship does not have the time to keep up with all the laws, find a tax professional who can help with your missionary's situation. One such organization that specializes in missionary taxes is Worth Tax Service, P.O. Box 725, Winona Lake IN 46590 USA. It is imperative that you or someone from your church leadership contact them or some other truly knowledgeable financial organization *before* you send your worker to the field—just to make sure all is in order in this vital area of logistics support.

Mary was just going to Hong Kong for two years. "I

won't be earning any money in the United States. I don't need to worry about taxes!" she thought. She discovered how wrong she had been when, after returning home, she got an invitation to explain why she hadn't filed her income tax forms for two years. Back taxes plus interest had her making painful payments for several years.

Or take Sue, who thought that because her church had written a letter, she didn't have to pay Social Security. Don't let your cross-cultural worker become a horror story of trouble with the government!

3) Health

Responsible church leadership will make sure their cross-cultural worker and his whole family are in good health—physically, emotionally, mentally and spiritually before they go to the field. Leadership must further see that their health care needs are met through an adequate monthly income or through the church's health insurance program.

Three considerations: 1) Will the church's policy cover your missionary family when they are out of the United States? 2) Is the cost of the premium higher than the cost of health care in the country to which they are going? 3) Is health care provided to expatriates by the host nation's medical program?

Definitely related to the health and well-being of your cross-cultural worker is his safety. What will you as a sending church do if your worker gets in trouble in his host culture? What if he is caught in the crossfire of a civil disturbance? What if the government is overthrown? What if your worker is kidnapped?

The list goes on. Some hard facts! But it is far better to have these issues thought out ahead of time and to have a plan of action in place than to wait for your worker's phone call from prison to begin thinking about such matters!

4) Death
Death is an inevitable fact of life. Yet this most emotionally charged event is sometimes totally unplanned for by a missionary's sending church. To clarify the necessary details, your fellowship must plan ahead.

It is generally accepted that the best place to be buried is where one dies. Many countries do not embalm; therefore they require burial within 24 hours.

The expense of immediate or even chartered flights out of a country are usually prohibitive. Furthermore, "He lived, he worked, he died and he is buried among us," is a powerful statement of the incarnation of Christ in your cross-cultural worker among a targeted people group. His testimony lives on!

A further, emotionally charged consideration is the expense of a field worker coming home for the funeral of a relative. Do you tell your missionary that you simply can't afford to fly him home to comfort his mother at his father's funeral because you weren't prepared? Will you take up a special offering for such an emergency? Do you maintain an emergency fund?

Carefully think through these and other life-and-death policies.

Attending to Personal Details
Beyond this array of details that are best handled by the mission agency and church leadership under their spiritual and corporate covering, there is a host of bits and pieces of logistical matters that can be handled by an individual. The list here merely suggests the innumerable situations that could arise with your particular field worker.

1) Material goods

If their car didn't sell before they left, you could hold power of attorney to sell it for them—at agreed-upon terms, of course. You could manage the rental or lease of their house or other properties. You could make payments from their bank account for property, insurance or other home-country financial commitments. You could send them the proper income tax forms, absentee ballots for elections, renewal of licenses forms, credentials or certificates. You could store their few boxes of personal belongings which they chose not to sell or take with them. And, of course, you could arrange to ship necessary materials to them on time!

2) Family matters

You may be called upon to be executor of your missionary's will. You may be asked to be the parents of their children if death should occur. You may be the ideal person to visit or care for their elderly parents. You may be able to provide a home for their college-age child attending school in your town. You may have the contacts to provide the home schooling curriculum materials they need. You may represent your missionary at family gatherings or events.

3) Ministry needs

You could gather and mail ministry items to your workers—Bibles, food and clothing for the poor, Sunday school materials and pictures. Since prices of many types of technical equipment is actually much lower in the USA, you could become your missionary's source for information and purchase of computers, modems, fax machines or hand-crank or solar-powered cassette players. You might research and expedite purchase of video and audio blank tapes and other supplies. Or you might put your goers in touch with sources from whom they may purchase directly.

These jobs only suggest the enormity and diversity of this important support role—the role of a *go-fer!* Members of your sending team with real gifts of service must attend to all your worker's responsibilities that continue in his home country.

Logistics support is essentially caring for each other in the Body of Christ. The Word teaches a simple doctrine: We really do need each other. We are the Family of God, The Body of Christ. Paul simply said that the Body should work together as a whole with all the members having the same care one for another (1 Corinthians 12:25).

Logistics support members must have certain qualifications:

Diligence: Sometimes it takes a bit of research to find all the correct income tax forms. Sometimes it takes some creative looking to find an inexpensive source or any source for New Testaments in the Uzbek language!

Concern for details: How to mail items—completing the customs forms, packaging, postage, labeling—takes time and communication with the field worker regarding mailing requirements in the host country and detailed concern in working with the US Postal Service or other carrier service.

New missionaries in Peru got a notice from the Lima post office that a package of homemade cookies had arrived from the States. When presented with an exorbitant import duty for the shipment, the missionaries decided they should pay it for the sake of their relationship with the well-meaning senders...until an experienced missionary told them the package would have been "accidentally" damaged and all the cookies would be gone anyway! Logistics support must be concerned with details such as import duties on care packages.

Punctuality: When you get a request for an item from your cross-cultural worker, chances are that a week or two has already passed since the need became acute. Finding what was requested, packaging and sending it—in addition to the return mail time—can cause quite a delay. Any procrastination increases the wait.

Sound business practices: Your record-keeping and promptness of payment in your missionary's financial dealings is a reflection of *their* integrity in business.

One missionary family turned the management of the rental of their house over to a friend. Bills and receipts accompanied every check that this friend wrote. The records were kept with accuracy. The businesslike manner of their friend gave them confidence that all would be well when they returned.

Be assured that the peace of mind that you as a good logistics support person can provide for a cross-cultural worker is equal in value to the things you do for him. What a privileged opportunity to serve as a sender!

Case Study in Logistics Support

The Core Group we have been following shows us more on this area of support:

> The logistics support we provide for Lou and Sandy includes legal aspects such as serving as executors and keepers of their wills. It also involves taking care of some of their financial affairs such as income tax and life insurance payments.

It has even included selling their car.

Lou and I were roommates in college and have managed to remain close friends ever since. It was this long-standing relationship that led Lou to ask me to take care of his business while he and Sandy were in the Philippines. It seemed like a simple task: Mail an occasional check, file a form or two.... It was—I thought—no big deal!

As Lou and Sandy prepared to go to a training course in Mexico, they were very busy and we never seemed to find the time to get together. We finally found one-half hour to discuss how they ran their lives, what bills they had due each month and how we were going to handle their financial affairs. Additionally, we met at their bank to put me as a signatory on their savings account and complete a power of attorney form to authorize me full control of their business affairs.

As I started paying their bills, I quickly realized that I needed a system to keep records of what I had paid. Thankfully my wife is much more organized than I and produced an old bill-organizer that is working fine. It will hopefully provide them a full accounting of what we have done when they return from the Philippines.

Taking over their financial affairs hasn't been easy. There have been those unexplained bills— like the $45 medical records check from a life insurance company. Do I pay this? I didn't know how to handle this one!

Then there was the car! "The Bomb," as Lou affectionately called it, was one of those things that gives used car salesmen such a bad reputation. Suddenly I found myself faced with having to sell a car I wouldn't wish on my worst enemy! Fortunately, a mechanic friend of Lou's was willing to take it as a "project" car.

The hardest part of what we are doing is the realization that we could really mess up someone else's business credibility, and that they are not in a position to do anything about it. It came to a head when we needed to find out if they wanted us to do their taxes or mail all the information to them. As the April 15 deadline approached, we realized that the mail would not go back and forth fast enough to communicate.

We checked with the phone company and found the cheapest times to call that would still fit into both our schedules. After trying to connect for half an hour, we prayed that if the decision we had come to about their taxes was wrong, we would get through the next time. The next time, Lou answered the phone! We *had* made the wrong decision and were able to straighten out a number of nagging questions. Our peace of mind—and theirs as well—only cost $15.

The lessons we logistics supporters have already learned on how to do this right include:

1) Sit down for several sessions with the couple you are sending. Even if they are going out under a well-known mission agency or association, don't presume that all their personal business matters will somehow be taken care of. Go over taxes, past and present. Discuss every financial obligation they have. Find out why they have these bills and why they pay them the way they do and whom to contact when questions arise.

2) Get a full, durable power of attorney for the husband and wife separately.

3) Set up a record-keeping system with the couple before they leave. Find out how they want their records maintained so that you don't just hand them a stack of old bills and cancelled checks when they return.

4) Make sure that their wills are complete and on file with their executor. If that is you, get a safety deposit box. Make sure they have expressed how they wish for their remains to be disposed of. Lou, being a very practical guy said, "The cheapest way possible!"

5) Pray about the responsibility you are about to accept. The enemy just loves to confuse and condemn anyone trying to do anything for the Lord—even something as simple (?) as paying a few bills!

This is logistics support at its best! There is no way of anticipating what your missionary will ask for; there is no knowing when a request will come. But one committed to the task and diligent in the work is a rare and prized partner in cross-cultural ministry. You may just be that person.

But for your missionary to sense the full support he needs, other areas of your possible service become important also. So that he may become "disentangled with the affairs of this life" and preach the Gospel freely, a vital part of the team becomes those who provide the *financial* support.

(In addition to the individual study below, see the **Group Leader's Guide** for session three beginning on page 188.)

For Your Personal Involvement

• Read Paul's account of cooperation in the Body of Christ from 1 Corinthians 12. Particularly note the care given to the "less comely" parts.

• In the Book of Acts, underline all references to travel logistics. With today's electronic communication systems, how could someone "back home" have helped in each of these instances?

• Make a list of all the things in your life that would need attention "back home" if you went away for two years. These are probably the things your missionary has to find someone to handle when he leaves.

Action Steps

By the time you have read Chapter Three, completed the *For Your Personal Involvement* section and participated in a group discussion, you should...

• Understand the potentially vast number of details involved in logistics support.

• Be more aware that we are the Body of Christ and we really do need each other.

• Decide whether God wants you to be on the Logistics Support Team of a cross-cultural worker you know. If so, write to him and inquire of any logistical needs that he may have. Make yourself available to assist in that need.

• Multiply yourself. As you come to understand the value of this type of support, encourage others to consider it as their place in the Body of Christ.

Chapter Four   Financial Support

"It has been a great joy to me that after all this time you have shown such interest in my welfare. I don't mean that you had forgotten me, but up till now you have had no opportunity of expressing your concern. Nor do I mean that I have been in actual need, for I have learned to be content, whatever the circumstances may be. I know now how to live when things are difficult and I know how to live when things are prosperous."

Philippians 4:10-12

"In totally miraculous ways God opened four major doors to bring us to Cameroon, West Africa, as Short-Term Assistants (STAs) with Wycliffe.

"Being STAs wasn't new to us. We had spent two eventful years in Mexico and later thought of serving again—sometime. But I had no idea returning to the field was the reason for an appointment at 8 a.m. one September morning with Dan Harrison, Wycliffe's Superintendent of Children's Education.

"But the longer we talked, the more I wondered if God wanted us on the field again—now! By 9:30 we decided I wasn't the one to go to Nepal; by 10:30 I had some reservations about Papua New Guinea; by 11:00 a.m. we were praying for God's direction for me to be a principal-teacher in Cameroon.

"'We're going to Africa!' I announced as I walked through the front door of our home that day. While my wife Jill and I prayerfully considered the decision, we knew God would have to open several doors which otherwise could keep us from going.

"The first one was regarding our oldest son James, who was only a semester away from graduation. Would it even be fair to him to change schools again? Though we definitely wanted him to go with us, it would have to be his decision. As days merged into weeks, his attitude changed from 'Do your own thing, but don't expect me to go,' to 'Let's get going!'

"Our home represented another obstacle. How could we ever find a family who would be totally responsible for the house for two years? But in God's time schedule He brought close friends to Southern California for a furlough from their ministry with Wycliffe in Mexico. They moved in—we moved out; leaving pictures on the walls and linens in the closet!

"A third problem was my mother-in-law's health. She was battling cancer and really depending on Jill for moral support. God took care of her needs through a miraculous healing!

"The fourth door to be opened had dollar signs on it! We learned that the cost of living in Cameroon was as high as in Southern California. We sent a letter to our friends—those who we thought would be interested in what we felt sure God wanted us to do. Money began coming in. A bonus on the job. A buyer for the car and travel trailer. Our church board had just decided to double its support for Wycliffe families. Friends pledged toward our monthly needs.

"We received official approval from the Wycliffe Board. Passports and immunizations were now in order. We were assured our visas would arrive between November 12 and 15. We set our departure date: 10 p.m. November 18 from the Los Angeles airport.

"All the normal hectic things were happening: We were trying to buy lightweight clothing in a winter market; packing, weighing, repacking; finding a misplaced birth certificate; sending out another letter; having the last gala round of visits with friends.

"Then November 18 came. At 8 a.m. I was making the final tally of our financial situation—a task I had intentionally delayed. I just couldn't make it all add up. We were $50 a month short.

"'I just cannot sign our Statement of Financial Preparedness,' I regretfully told Jill. We all laughed at the ridiculousness of our situation. Luggage filled the living room. The kids were checked out of school. Our car was sold. Our friends were already living with us—and wanted us to get out of their house! All goodbyes had been said. We were holding $3000 of non-redeemable airline tickets in our hands. We'd radioed Africa that we were on our way. And here we were, $50 a month short of our support goal!

"'The Lord must be planning to send in some money today,' I said as I put the statement aside, unsigned.

"At 9 a.m. Jill's mother called, asking if we needed any money. She then related an incredible story about Myrna, a lady in my father-in-law's church. She had been on our financial support team during our time with Wycliffe in Mexico. And she had heard us present the financial needs for this new venture in Cameroon. Unknown to us, she had been struggling for several weeks for a way in which God could use her again on our financial support team.

"But it was now the night before we were to leave. Myrna spent a sleepless vigil asking the Lord for some way that she could still help us. Their business was in financial difficulties and their house had just been robbed. At 4 a.m. she dozed off and at 7 a.m. was up preparing to go to a church missions meeting. At 8 a.m. (while I was doing my figuring) she put on a coat she hadn't worn since the previous winter. She put her hand in the pocket and, to her amazement, drew out $1,200 in cash! The thief who had so thoroughly gone through her husband's clothing in that closet three nights before had completely missed her coat!

"This is for the Coopers!' she shouted. 'Thank you, Lord, for Your faithfulness!'

"I said, 'Praise the Lord!' The $1,200 she found in the pocket and wanted us to have was exactly the $50 support for 24 months that we lacked. I ran for the Statement of Financial Preparedness and signed, 'Yes, we are ready to go!'"

Financial support is the most controversial, thus the most talked-about of the six areas of support. In fact, when you mention missionary support, most people think of nothing else but money.

We walk through the marketplaces of the Christian world, confronted by a spectrum of contradictions. On the one hand, we are made to feel guilty by the millions who are starving to death because we do not give $15 to such-and-such an organization. On the other extreme, we are told "Prosperity is your divine right!" Where do we turn for balance in financial responsibility?

To further complicate the issue is the problem that a god of this age in America is materialism. The United States, representing only 5% of the world's population, consumes 40% of the earth's manufactured goods and 70% of all petroleum products. In addition, the media creates, then preys on society's poor self-image by saying, "You aren't good enough...until you use our product!" So we endlessly toil to purchase this and that, only to find out in the next commercial that a "new and improved" version is now available. As the bumper sticker says, "I owe, I owe, so off to work I go!" How do we rise above the trivia of this world to see financial responsibility from God's perspective?

His Word, of course, communicates His perspective. On the stub of every pay check received by Christians could be the words of Deuteronomy 8:17-18: "Remember the Lord your God, for it is He who gives you the ability to produce wealth." Recently a primetime news program noted, "The average salary of an American Christian is greater than that of a non-Christian." The newscaster's commentary was, "So that's what those Christians are always praying about!"

Eight out of every ten dollars held by Christians in the world are in the hands of American Christians! As we hold this wealth, then, we must ask the next question: "*Why* has He so blessed His people in America?" Again, the Word gives a clear answer: "God be merciful to us and bless us and cause Your face to shine upon us *so that* Your way may be known on earth and Your salvation among all nations" (Psalm 67:1-2). God's principle that His people are blessed to be a blessing is established in the covenant He made with Abraham (see Genesis 12).

Some of the more familiar methods of securing finances to bless the world through cross-cultural outreach ministry include bake sales and car washes, newspaper drives and aluminum recycling. And in an increasingly waste-conscious economy, these endeavors do generate some working capital. A neighborhood garage sale with all or a portion of the proceeds going to a missions project or missionary can bring families together for good causes. Arts and crafts items can be made and sold and again the profit given to a missionary. God blesses us with ingenuity, mouth-watering recipes and entrepreneurial skills so that we can financially bless the spread of His Kingdom.

But the time will come when all garages are clean, people will want to keep their remaining newspapers to light the winter fires and everybody has had their fill of fundraising pizzas.

More likely, the time will come when your cross-cultural outreach ministry has grown beyond the funds that can be generated by these methods. And now diligent effort must be made to look beyond these endeavors to some more creative, long-lasting ways of securing finances for cross-cultural outreach ministry. Let's look at three areas of biblical stewardship: giving, lifestyle and managing wealth.

Giving

We know the Word: God loves a cheerful giver. It is more blessed to give than to receive. Give, and it shall be given unto you. When you give.... Yet the brilliance of the Bible's simple teaching on the principle of giving invariably gets around to "how much" which inevitably leads to tithing which ultimately deals with the nitty-gritty of "Do I tithe on my net or on my gross?" And we have run into the same dead end the Jews had when Jesus said to them: "You pay tithe of mint and dill and cummin, but omit the weightier matters of the Law.... You strain out the gnat and swallow the camel!" (Matthew 23:23-24).

The discipline of tithing (which Jesus commended the Jews for doing) leads a Christian to a deeper commitment of "generous, cheerful, hilarious" giving (2 Corinthians 9:7) which grows into the willing mind principle of 2 Corinthians 8:12-14: "That there may be an equality!"

Using this principle, as long as we compare ourselves only to those wealthier than we are, we don't feel too compelled to give. But when we enlarge our vision to encompass the world, the principle of equality has us giving and giving some more since the poverty level in

America is in the top 4% of world family income. We are indeed rich in finances.

A hymn of the Church says: "I surrender all, I surrender all. All to Jesus I surrender; I surrender all." May we, in our responsible stewardship of finances, grapple with God's Word and the work of the Holy Spirit in our lives to that point of full surrender.

Before we go on, let's back up to the basic concept: If every Christian in your fellowship tithed, that tithe would keep the finance committee busy meeting every week to determine its disbursement!

None of us likes to hear a 20-minute sermon on giving before each offering in taken. But the very concept of "taking" an offering instead of "freely you have received, freely give" (Matthew 10:8) might be educating us to be miserly in our giving. Sometimes even the prayer said at offering time does more to support our meager giving than encourage a "generous, cheerful, hilarious" freewill gift: "Father, You know we only have these few pennies to give to You. But You multiply them so the whole world can believe in You!" And we put our wallets away and pull out our loose change—if we have any!

Or we are taught to "pay" our tithes. As with any other bill, therefore, a conscious or unconscious resentment can develop. Rather, the Bible urges that God's people "bring all the tithes into the storehouse" (Malachi 3:10). "Lay up for yourselves treasures in Heaven, where moth and rust don't corrupt" (Matthew 6:20). That sounds more like securing a sound investment than "paying a bill." And that grows into, "What a privilege that God would allow me to be a part of His Plan of the Ages. He could get along without my money, for 'He owns the cattle on a thousand hills' (Psalm 50:10). But the Lord is giving me an opportunity to invest in His Kingdom!"

Giving is an act of intelligent worship. "Let every

man who will do it willingly from his heart bring Me an offering" (Exodus 25:2). "Every man shall give as he is able" (Deuteronomy 16:17). "Every man according to his ability determined to send relief" (Acts 11:29). "But first there must be a willing mind" (2 Corinthians 8:12). "Let every one give as he has purposed in his heart" (2 Corinthians 9:7). What do we learn from His Word? That generous, cheerful, hilarious giving is not an awkward interruption to worship, but the very essence of it.

How can we be wise about our giving?

Unfortunately, not all individuals and organizations vying for your support dollars are themselves wise stewards. There are three questions you must ask to check them on their accountability:

1) Is the money you give going for what they say it is? Do they take 60 cents of your dollar to raise additional funds? A dedicated sender once gave $30,000 to an international project. A year later, the ones who had solicited this gift came back to him, apologizing that they had not used the money as they had told him. Would he forgive them? Did he want his money back? An apology doesn't happen often! More likely the funds are hidden in the language of the bookkeeper's report!

2) Is the project or missionary service really hitting a decisive point of battle for souls? God wants us to be a part of ministries that yield "fruit that remains."

You might even have to say "no" to your closest friend's appeal if you sense his summer of service sounds more like a surf and sun holiday!

Worthwhile missionary service is as diverse as the creative genius of God flowing through His obedient servants. And some of the activities seem 'way out there— somewhere! But if they are really hitting a decisive point of battle for the souls of mankind, there will be a line of correlation that can be traced to "fruit that remains."

3) If your cross-cultural worker is going out through a US-based organization, what is the US administrative/ field use ratio of the mission's funds? That is, how much is spent in the States to get one dollar to the field? Is it under 20%? Are the US personnel living on a comparable level to their field workers? How do they raise their finances? (By the way, if an organization doesn't want to answer this type of question, you have a pretty good idea of their accountability already!) God owns all; yet He is the most frugal economist! ACMC (formerly Association of Church Mission Committees) offers a battery of appropriate questions for you to ask a missions agency with which you are considering developing a relationship (see "Resources," page 203).

Lifestyle
Statistics can bore or shock or motivate. For example: Americans spend as much on chewing gum in a year as they give to missions. Americans pay as much for pet food in 52 days as they spend annually on missions. On one day, February 14, Americans spend $700 million to say, "I love you" with Valentines Day cards. Less than that is spent in the whole month of February (and each of the other months) to tell a lost and dying world that God loves them! Does our lifestyle, as Jesus said, tell us where our heart is?

The huge cruise ship the Queen Mary was designed as a luxury vessel; yet during World War II it was converted to serve as a troop carrier. Today the museum aboard the Queen Mary affords a stunning contrast between the lifestyles appropriate in peace and war. On one side of a partition, the tables prepared for high society hold a dazzling array of dishes, crystal and silver.

On the other side, one metal tray with indentations replaces 15 dishes and saucers. Bunks, eight tiers high, accommodate 15,000 troops in contrast to the 3,000 wealthy patrons in peacetime transport. To so drastically reconstruct the vessel took a national emergency. The survival of a nation depended upon it. Should you replace your china with metal trays? No! But allow the Holy Spirit to challenge every aspect of your lifestyle.

Our Master calls out, "Rescue the perishing!" The Captain of the Lord of Hosts has trumpeted a certain sound for battle. But the cry of the perishing is often lost in the din of self-survival. While pursuing comfort we can easily ignore Christ's warning in Scripture, "He who would seek to save his life will lose it" (Luke 17:33). We decry the diseases of the underdeveloped nations: tuberculosis, malnutrition, parasites, typhoid and others. Yet America has virtually invented a whole new set of affluence-related diseases: obesity, arteriosclerosis, heart disease, strokes, lung cancer, venereal disease, cirrhosis of the liver and more. In saving ourselves we are well on our way to losing ourselves! (See "Resources," page 200.)

Any good cross-cultural training teaches the missionary to adapt as much as possible to the lifestyle of those he is going to minister among—a simpler lifestyle, a lowered consumption of goods, a make-do and/or seek-a-creative-alternative attitude. This forms a solid principle of bonding—establishing a sense of belonging with the ones he serves.

Those who serve as senders might experience a new sense of belonging and a new vision of their part in rescuing the perishing if they, too, would adopt a lifestyle that approximates that of those they are sending. Senders who take on this challenge often find that somehow their *quality* of life usually improves.

A diligent financial support team member must allow the radical challenges of these statements to question his lifestyle:

1) If my lifestyle runs out of money before the month runs out of days, a humbling but good starting point might be for me to ask for help in personal financial management.

2) If my lifestyle looks into a five-foot-long closet of clothes and doesn't see "a thing to wear," possibly a new reading of "Do not be anxious about what clothes you will put on, for the body is more than clothing" (Luke 12:22-23) might give me a new perspective on the situation.

3) If my lifestyle demands a status symbol for transportation, I should check carefully Christ's story of "bigger barns" (Luke 12:16-21).

4) If my lifestyle builds long hallways and huge bedrooms and bathrooms for each family member and a living room family room, recreation room and parlor, it might be well for me to consider my Christian longings for a home in the city "whose builder and maker is God" (Hebrews 11:10).

5) If my lifestyle careens on the roller coasters of thrills and frills, it might be well for me to turn down the speed and volume enough to notice that life is ready to give free excitement and exhilaration through natural beauty (Psalm 19:1-3), fellowship, contemplation and worship.

As we prayerfully consider the Holy Spirit's dealing in our life, we will yield to His will. For "He who has begun a good work in you will bring it to completion" (Philippians 1:6; also see Philippians 2:12 and 13).

God's direction regarding finances is not one-size-fits-all. There is no hint that Jesus ever told Mary, Martha and Lazarus to sell any of their wealth. And the record suggests they were quite well-to-do. Yet to the rich young ruler, He said, "Sell all" (Matthew 19:21).

Although many Christian finance books only make us feel guilty or tell us to tighten our belts, an excellent book on this subject is *Living More With Less* by Doris Janzen Longacre (see "Resources," page 200). It contains literally hundreds of practical lifestyle changes that encompass every aspect of finance. And it assures you of an enhanced way of life.

Christians with a renewed lifestyle can free up thousands—even millions—of creative dollars for cross-cultural ministry. Living more with less is an exciting, viable option.

Managing Wealth

No more than a cursory glance at the parable of the talents (Matthew 25:14-30) assures us that the Lord expects us to be wise in managing the wealth He has entrusted to us. In a related parable in Luke 19:11-27, He tells us to "occupy—be about My work in a businesslike manner—until I come."

We can exercise Christian stewardship on two levels: financial practices on the field and financial resources behind the lines.

Financial Practices On The Battlefield

• Missionaries could implement plans that include short term, itinerant, Pauline-style assignments instead of strategies that demand costly real estate or other long-term investment. Admittedly, some cross-cultural assignments require a very long commitment—Bible translation, for one. But many mission assignments could be turned over to nationals sooner than they are so that your missionary could move on to new areas of need. A sad but valid criticism is that many jobs still being done by missionaries could be handled more effectively by nationals! Notice Paul's strong encouragement to Titus to "appoint elders in every city" (see Titus 1:5).

His further note, quoting Crete's own poet, suggests Titus was having a hard time finding qualified men—but he was to get on with it! (Titus 1:12).

• Another practice of biblical times was to move (for one reason or another) to a new area, become a resident of that country and seek employment (see Acts 18:1-19 for the example of Aquila and Priscilla). In some situations your missionary could do this and release his funds for others.

• Making a greater use of tentmaker opportunities gets your missionary living and working with the people. Teaching English as a second language is one of the best opportunities; becoming an international student is a close second. But beyond these are thousands of jobs around thc world that would allow your missionary to get *Out of the Saltshaker and Into the World* as a book by Rebecca Pippert challenges. There are some serious considerations, however, that must be given to this type of ministry. Don Hamilton's book *Tentmakers Speak Out* is particularly helpful reading in this area (see "Resources," page 200).

• Self-support by independently wealthy or retired people is becoming a more viable option to financial support. With our increasing senior citizen population, agencies are specifically recruiting these people.

• Team-oriented housing instead of single-family dwellings may free needed funds. Perhaps a mission team house right in the community of the targeted people would be wise. The Word became flesh and dwelt among us; we touched Him and He was touched by our feelings (see John 1:14; 1 John 1:1; Hebrews 4:15). Jesus was a powerful example of living with the people.

• The greater use of non-Western workers and methods is a fast-growing trend as God is sovereignly raising up a "new wave" of missionary thrust. It is coming from Third World nations. Missionaries from America can work with this move of God! "Fruit that remains" is our goal. How is this most effectively accomplished? Paul, that great missionary statesman of the 1st century serves as an excellent model—again!

He was an evangelist. Most often we read of his preaching the Gospel. (There were only a few exceptions—the most notable one being his several years in Ephesus.) However, he did have a team of teachers (Timothy and Titus are the best known, but there were many others—see Acts 20:4) who were left behind to find faithful men—nationals—and teach them the Word in such a way that they would go out to teach others (2 Timothy 2:2).

If you are in a position to formulate policy or financially support missionaries, be a wise and faithful steward. Study and network with mission strategists about wise financial policies. Don't establish a ministry that must be forever subsidized by Western money after being turned over to nationals. Don't teach to nationals discipling methods that require anything not easily accessible in their culture—movie projectors, big buildings or perhaps *any* buildings, expensive books, vehicles, etc. Do let the simplicity of the Gospel be clothed in the nationals' own cultural garb.

There are additional ways of saving missionary dollars. They are found in how we manage His wealth entrusted to us back home.

Financial Resources Behind The Lines
• Cooperatives. A Christian co-op offers extensive possibilities to manage the wealth God has given us. Share, Inc. of San Diego, California, now receiving na-

tional publicity as a model, is a community project with a vision for feeding the poor. It could as easily be adapted for any noble cause. Whether in the area of food or clothing, household items or services, a Christian co-op is an excellent way to free up finances for the advancement of the Kingdom.

• Thrift stores. In the 1st century, Christians had "all things in common" (Acts 4:32). Today we can share our excess goods by letting others buy them through a thrift store. It could be totally supplied by free goods and operated by volunteers. (Probably one paid manager to keep it operating smoothly would be good.) Well-managed, this type of business could give its proceeds to missions.

There are, of course, government regulations. And it would require diligent business practices. But the rewards of funding more field workers or study Bibles for national pastors or church-planting teams is well worth the energy.

• Multi-level sales. These businesses continue to capture the market of distribution of goods. It is said that if growth continues at its present rate, by the year 2000, 50% of all products will be purchased by this means. In choosing a company, it is essential to identify with one that is selling a marketable product and one whose quality and cost is competitive with traditional marketing. Some organizations will allow an entire non-profit group to enter the "down line."

• Mutual fund investing. It is not known just what markets the stewards traded in in the parable of the talents. But it is impossible that they just "put it in the bank." The master would have had to be gone on a very long journey to double the money even at 10% interest.

And the unfaithful steward was reprimanded for not at least doubling his money (see Matthew 25:14-30). You probably know or know those who know how to bring the surpluses of your fellowship together in mutual fund investing (with agreed-upon security and other details that need to be carefully worked out).

• Estate planning. This source of funds holds good, long-term money available for Kingdom work. Unfortunately, it is a method already being abused by some Christian organizations. Nonetheless, it is an area in which we have been called upon to be faithful stewards. Millions of dollars per year go into state coffers because about 60% of our population dies without a will! This area does require a knowledgeable consultation. But generating mission funds through estate planning can be done in good taste, and for His glory.

• Grant funding. Another whole source of money for warfare against the enemy lies in the estates of certain philanthropic individuals and societies. Yes, it is a lot of work to write the proposals. Yes, many more will say no than yes, but literally millions of dollars are available for the right group doing the right thing and having written the right proposal.

• Matching funds. It is an accepted and growing practice of industry and individuals to "match funds" for worthy causes. This has been employed mostly in gifts to educational institutions. However, the tax benefit to the company is the same whether to one non-profit organization or another. It would probably work best to name some specific project in a Third World country.

Do you know a retired banker or other financial manager whose dealings with money are keen with years of experience? Nudge him to put those skills to the

Master's use in managing these types of financial resources. Maybe that person is you!

• Income tax. Some people claim "no deductions," allowing the government to use their money all year interest free just so they can use the "forced savings" in their refund. How much better would be the disciplined saving of that amount—at least at bank rates! At the end of the year (or quarter), pay the government its due and give the interest earned to your cross-cultural worker's support fund.

• Equity. If you have owned real property for some years, the equity could be put out at interest to generate dollars for cross-cultural ministry.

Get financial counsel about any of these suggestions from trustworthy people who understand money well. Also, there are journals you can study. And there is the Holy Spirit to guide your bold actions to free up creative dollars for cross-cultural outreach ministry.

World economic crises are daily in our news: OPEC nations at a conference table in the Middle East affect gasoline prices in the West. High consumption nations import cheap products from economically impoverished countries, while sending back ever-higher-priced manufactured goods. International companies buy land to produce export crops, forcing local people to pay higher prices on imported food. Producers dump a million tons of grain in the ocean to maintain marketable prices.

On a scale far greater than we can comprehend, many Christians ignorantly or glibly contribute to the economic injustice of the world, shrugging off any responsibility with a simple "What can one person do?" God's response is in the singular: "But whoever has the world's goods and sees his brother in need, and hardens his heart against him, how does the love of God abide in him?" (1 John 3:17). Or, for even stronger words from our Lord, read Proverbs 24:11-12!

In all of the areas we have considered, the influence of one person is small. But it is one by one that we will stand before Him and give an accounting of our actions: "Wood, hay, stubble" or "gold, silver and precious stones!" (1 Corinthians 3:12-13).

We are to become "faithful...in the unrighteous riches" so that the Lord will "commit to our trust the true riches" (Luke 16:1-12).

A Case Study in Financial Support

The team of senders we have been following are able to rejoice in this area of support:

Because Lou and Sandy were our church's missionaries, we felt that there was a minimum amount of monthly support that needed to be raised by us before we went outside our fellowship for financial support. Early on, Lou had challenged all potential Core Group members to financially support this mission as concrete evidence of ownership.

Financial support as well as prayer, moral and communication support was raised in this way: First our fellowship was made aware of Lou and Sandy's vision. One Sunday, Lou presented a slide show of a trip he and Sandy had taken to the Philippines several months before to see firsthand several ministry opportunities offered to them.

For the next three Sundays after his presentation, the fellowship inserted into the church bulletin a commitment form with several boxes to check, including:

1) a commitment to support them financially with a space for how much and whether it was a one-time gift or monthly;

2) a commitment to support them in prayer;

3) a commitment to support them with letters.

We had a poster made with the "Good Ship L, S & M" at one side. It was moveable and acted as the financial "thermometer." The "ship" moved weekly toward its destination as commitment forms came in for Lou, Sandy and Marlies.

Once the minimum amount of support was raised (an amount determined by the agency they would be working under), Lou and Sandy then went to family and friends outside our fellowship for financial support.

After all support was committed, support packages were assembled and sent to each contributor. The packet contained:

1) A photo magnet of their family to put on the refrigerator.

2) A "Coupon Book" with a two-year supply (this was the length of their commitment) of coupons that included the month and a space for the amount of support—much like a loan coupon book from a bank!

3) Twenty-four envelopes with our church's mailing address already affixed for easy mailing.

So far most everyone has been great about keeping up with their monthly support. Each month our church sends a check to the organization's home office. From there the money is telexed to Lou and Sandy. We've been very blessed! Our fellowship has been so willing to support financially that we haven't had to come up with any unusual or emergency means to secure finances for them.

Praise the Lord!

What a blessing it is when people give of their substance so that His Good News can go forth. But there is more to the full measure of support needed by your cross-cultural worker. The nickname given to James (the brother of our Lord) was "camel-knees" from all the time he spent in prayer. Consider the concert of prayer you can offer to God on behalf of your worker.

(In addition to the individual study below, see the **Group Leader's Guide** for session four beginning on page 189.)

For Your Personal Involvement

• Paul had quite a bit to say about his financial support (or lack thereof)! Read each of the following passages and try to determine Paul's philosophy regarding financial support: 1 Corinthians 9; 2 Corinthians 12:13-19; Philippians 4:10-19; Philemon 18-22.

• Do an Old and New Testament word study on tithing. Discover that it is a principle of God's Kingdom that works! Include Abraham's refusal to receive money from the king of Sodom, yet he himself gave a tithe to Melchizedek, King of Salem (Genesis 14; Hebrews 7:1-2).

• Without changing your spending patterns, for one month keep a detailed record of every expenditure you make. Then prayerfully begin listing areas in your lifestyle where there might possibly be unnecessary expenditures. Use the five statements on page 82 to challenge you in this activity.

• Name several commercial jingle phrases that if followed could easily distract you from giving financial support to your missionary. What are you going to do to combat the impact of materialism in your life?

Action Steps
By the time you have read Chapter Four, completed the *For Your Personal Involvement* section and participated in a group discussion, you should...

• Decide to purchase Doris Longacre's book *Living More With Less.* Read and apply it!

• Plan to attend a Christian financial management seminar in your area.

• Prepare a will or living trust.

• Know if you are to be a part of a missionary's Financial Support Team. If yes, let him know of your commitment. Find out where and how to send your check. Let him know the amount the Lord has put on your heart.

• Multiply yourself. Look for others who have their finances in order and wish to see their funds used for Kingdom work.

Chapter Five   Prayer Support

"Praying always with all prayer and supplication in the Spirit."

Ephesians 6:18a

In 1923 Helen Mollenkof, a pretty teenager, attended a Keswick Conference in New Jersey. The speaker was L. L. Legters, who along with Cameron Townsend many years later would found Wycliffe Bible Translators.

God had given Legters a deep burden for all the indigenous people of Mexico and Central America without the Bible in their language. Speaking at the Keswick Conference, he challenged the young people to take the name of one language group in Mexico and pray for that people—that God would open the doors so His Word could be translated into the language of their heart.

Helen Mollenkof was one of those who answered the challenge. She stepped forward and picked the name of a people she'd never heard of before: the Mazahua. She wrote the name on the flyleaf of her Bible. Then, closing her eyes, this teen-aged girl promised the Lord she would pray for them until they had the Bible translated into their own language.

Helen went ahead with life. She graduated from school, became a nurse and joined the Women's Union Missionary Society. Then she was sent to India, where she served as a missionary for the next thirty-five years. One of her ongoing prayer concerns was for the Mazahua people.

In 1967 Helen returned to the States to retire in Lancaster, Pennsylvania. Some time later, for some unexplained reason, she felt free to stop praying for the Mazahua people.

Then in 1981 she picked up her local newspaper and read an interview with Pat Hamric who, like herself, was a long-term missionary. As she read she discovered to her amazement that Pat along with Hazel Spotts and Don and Shirley Stewart had been Bible translators among the Mazahua people.

Overjoyed, she found Pat's address and wrote to her: "I thought you might be interested in my contact with the Mazahua Indians through prayer."

She told Pat about the Keswick meeting, how L. L. Letgers had challenged them to take the name of one language group in Mexico, and her commitment to pray.

Pat replied, "The New Testament is complete. It was dedicated in January of 1970!"

Helen realized that January 1970 was the very time the Lord lifted her burden to pray!

Most of us are aware of the significance of prayer in God's global plan. We have powerful articles and books on the topic: *An Army of Intercessors; A Concert of Prayer; Seven Minutes with God; Mountain Movers; Praying the Four Ways Christ Taught; Power in Prayer; Destined for the Throne; Effective Prayer Life; Touch the World through Prayer; With Christ in the School of Prayer.*

What is the sum of their message? In the words of Augustine, "Without God, we cannot; but without us, God will not."

In His sovereignty, God has voluntarily linked Himself to human cooperation. He has inextricably bound

Himself to the prayer of faith of His children. He merges His working with man's praying.

Though this is a deep mystery, it is clearly revealed in the Word and throughout history. Joshua's day in battle would have gone poorly without Moses' prayer (Exodus 17). Jacob's place in Israel's history would not have been the same without Peniel (Genesis 32). The cross would have been intolerable without Gethsemane (Luke 22).

Today one can stand in the bedroom where John Wesley and the members of the "Holy Club" held their prayer meetings, a force God used to ignite a revival that was felt around the world.

Consider Evan Roberts and his friends prostrating themselves before the Lord night after night, resulting in the Welsh Revival. Today the Prayer Mountain in Seoul, Korea gives impetus to the growth of several of the largest churches in the world. The revival sweeping Brazil is evidenced by extra police being put on duty to control traffic in several major cities on *prayer meeting* night!

In no greater arena of human activity is this mysterious union of our prayer and God's work seen than in the mission of the Church.

Jesus was going about all the cities and villages, teaching in their synagogues and preaching the Gospel of the Kingdom, but when He saw the multitudes, He was moved with compassion. Then He said to His disciples, "The harvest is great, but the laborers are few. Therefore, *pray* to the Lord of the harvest to send forth laborers into His harvest." Three verses later, He sent *them* out two by two (Matthew 9-10)!

At the end of time, Christ the Lamb will be extolled: "You were slain and have redeemed us to God by Your blood out of *every kindred and tongue and people and nation*" (Revelation 5:9). The twenty-four elders singing this new song will be holding golden vials full of incense which are the *prayers* of saints!

Paul in his masterful Ephesians 6 discourse on spiritual warfare not only clearly delineates the armor for our protection in war, but also identifies two of the major weapons of our warfare: the Sword of the Spirit and *prayer*.

As a missionary of the first century, he was continually calling on the churches for prayer support: "Brethren, pray for us" he simply stated in 1 and 2 Thessalonians and Hebrews. His appeal to the Christians in Rome seemed a bit more pressing: "I beseech you, brethren...that you *strive* together with me in your prayers to God for me" (Romans 15:30). Paul assumed Philemon was on his prayer support team (Philemon 22). To the church in Philippi, he stated his confidence that what he was experiencing would turn out well because of their prayers and the resources of the Spirit of Jesus Christ (Philippians 1:19)—bringing us back to that insoluble cooperation of God and man in prayer.

In spite of all of her lamentable weaknesses, appalling failures and indefensible shortcomings, the Church is the mightiest—the only—force that is contesting Satan's rule in human affairs! And that Church on her knees is the purifying and preserving influence which has kept the fabric of all we call civilization from total disintegration, decay and despair.

Samuel Chadwick said, "The one concern of the devil is to keep Christians from praying. He fears nothing from prayerless studies, prayerless work and prayerless religion. He laughs at our toil, mocks at our wisdom, but trembles when we pray!"

Prayer is not begging God to do something He is loathe to do. It is not overcoming God's reluctance to act. It is, rather, enforcing Christ's victory over Satan. It is the effective, fervent communication with the Creator of the Universe—in line with His will—which controls the balance of power in world affairs.

Prayer transcends the dimensions of time and space and ushers us into the very throne room of God, worshiping, petitioning and interceding in that spiritual realm of the eternal now.

Prayer is sometimes *alleluia* (Psalm 150). It is sometimes telling God the details of our *needs* (Philippians 4:6). It is sometimes laboring in unutterable groans of *intercession* (Romans 8:26). It is the prayer of a sending church that releases power through His messengers in China, Africa, Europe and Latin and North America.

Prayer is the arena of spiritual warfare. Those who enter there are in touch with a world in need. Those who enter there regularly know the scars but also the victory of battle.

Prayer is where the action is—supporting and sustaining those on the fields of the world.

It is vitally important for your cross-cultural worker to have a strong prayer support team every step of the way: from his calling to his planning, training, securing financial support and preparing to leave—all before he even arrives on the field.

All Christians are involved in spiritual warfare. Wherever they are aggressively battling the enemy, there is a greater vulnerability to his attacks. However, your cross-cultural worker often has to deal with battle tactics less familiar than those he faced back home. Where there is less Christian witness, there is greater oppression. Cultures more open to Eastern religions and animism are also more aware of the evil spirit world. Territory that Satan has held for generations does not yield easily. Add to this your worker's adjusting to all the unknowns of his new culture, and you already have a sizable prayer list.

However, because you may not have ever "been there," his prayer needs may seem so remote, so unreal. Thus, you may sense a lack of being able to make your prayer specific for him.

Here is a prayer list to give you a good start in understanding the areas of need peculiar to a cross-cultural worker that make him vulnerable to discouragement. When you communicate with him, ask which of these areas are vital to him. And as you let him know of your commitment to sustain him in prayer, he will be happy to keep you informed of the more specific requests.

• Adjusting to the new language, different foods, new customs, hard climate.

• Protection in travel, health, accidents, dangerous situations.

• Parents' concern for their children's health, schooling, friendships. Housing accommodations, lack of privacy, differences in living standards, lack of accustomed conveniences.

• Loneliness, homesickness, lack of accustomed fellowship with others.

• Interpersonal relationships, dealing with one's own (and others') prejudice, selfishness, depending on the faithfulness of others to meet one's financial needs.

• Effectiveness in ministry, whatever the assignment.

• Functioning of the tools of ministry. (It is amazing how printing presses break down just when a completed New Testament is ready for printing!)

• Lack of visible results; the "plowing, planting and watering" stages can go on for years!

• The people being ministered to, the national Christians, the leaders of the country.

• Need for stability, wisdom, compassion, self-discipline, boldness, power, love, to be filled with the Spirit of God.

A Model Prayer
Jo Shetler had completed the translation of the Balangao New Testament. A flourishing church had been established. She was now called back to the Philippines to

be a speaker at the Balangao Bible Conference. Her subject was prayer.

She said that her prayer life had consisted of "...all we ask God to do, such as heal our sicknesses, provide money to put children through school, give the ability to learn a language, translate Scripture and interact well with people.

"Then I decided to pray the prayers of Paul, David, and others in the Bible. I copied them out and started in. Wow, did I ever get a surprise! Those people weren't asking God for the same things I was! These 'model prayers' from Scripture seemed to center more directly on God and His program, rather than on people and their plans."

Read all the articles on prayer; read all the books about prayer. But when you are done, *study and pray* the prayers of the Bible!

One of the prayers of Paul fits perfectly the needs of the cross-cultural worker. He was praying it for the Christians in Colosse, but note how adaptable it is to the needs of any missionary.

Even before he prays, Paul twice assures those at Colosse that he is constantly praying for them. Look at Colossians 1:4,9: "praying always for you...; for this cause we also, since the day we heard of it, do not cease to pray for you."

Everyone who is interested in your missionary will at one time or another breathe a prayer for him. Certainly the Financial Support Team will pray as they write out their checks: "Lord, may they use this money wisely," or "Lord, do they really need this money more than I do?"

The Communication Support Team will no doubt pray that the letters they put so much time into will arrive safely and minister to your missionary.

The Moral Support Team will surely whisper a prayer as they see your missionary's picture on the church bulletin board or when the pastor leads in a congregational prayer for him.

But if you are going to be a part of your missionary's Prayer Support Team, your commitment must be more on the level of Paul's statement: "For this cause, we also since the day we heard of it, do not cease to pray for you."

Here, then, is a "model prayer" that you can pray for your cross-cultural worker:

"That you might be filled with the knowledge of His will..." (Colossians 1:9).

Once a worker arrives on the field, he is bombarded with an overwhelming array of ministry opportunities. Even if a predetermined job description has been established, there is always one more assignment to fit into the schedule. Joining a team that is short-handed by illness, furlough, or lack of laborers for an expanding ministry, every cross-cultural worker is faced with appeals to take on "just a little bit more."

Out of that mass of good deeds, your worker must discern those that were "beforehand determined that he should walk in" (Ephesians 2:10).

Once he has heard God's will, a corollary prayer is for him to judiciously share with his supervisor that, in order to maintain his sanity, he must say "no" to certain opportunities.

"...in all wisdom and spiritual understanding..." (Colossians 1:9).

It is noteworthy that throughout Scripture these two qualities of the Christian life are always twins—one with the other. *Wisdom* can be defined as "the ability to see things from God's perspective" and *understanding* as "the facility to make that godly perspective work out in the affairs of this world."

One missionary statesman wisely said, "The only ones who know everything about missions are those who have been on the field *less* than six months!" Bombarded with cultural distinctives, worlds apart from his own culture, and quite possibly faced with methods that have become rutted in tradition, your worker needs to continually see things from God's perspective—things pertaining to his family life, his ministry, his relationship with nationals, his economy of time and energy, his finances, his personal devotions, his relationships with ministers on his team and those of other groups.

It is not for nothing that Solomon urges: "Get wisdom, and with all your getting, get understanding!" (Proverbs 4:7).

As your prayers "bind the strong man" (Matthew 12:29) so your worker can have a clear vision from God's vantage point of eternal values—as your prayers elevate your missionary to be "seated with Christ in heavenly places" (Ephesians 2:6), he must now understand how to make all of that happen in the day-to-day affairs of his life.

Days—even weeks—of extended travel away from home wreak havoc with scheduled family time. Dare we use God's money to take a vacation? How do I tell the nationals that we aren't going to use US dollars to build their building—that it is better for the congregation to trust God for the provision? How do I not violate my doctrinal distinctives, yet develop a working relationship with others in the Body of Christ? These and a thousand questions bombard your worker's life and demand an understanding heart (see 1 Kings 3:9). To see things from God's perspective is one thing (wisdom); to know how to make them work out in your missionary's day-to-day life is another (understanding).

You can see how this prayer for wisdom and understanding could consume hours of intercession as you do war against the enemy.

***"That you might walk worthy of the Lord unto all pleasing"* (Colossians 1:10).**

Phillips' translation puts it, "That your outward lives which men see may bring credit to your Master's Name." Watchman Nee said, "If you want to be a missionary to China, plan on wearing a 'learner's permit' around your neck for the first *ten* years!" Because of diverse cultural distinctives and your cross-cultural worker's lack of ability to communicate deeply, it is often only the love of Christ working out through his life that tells the Gospel message.

Another perspective of this, of course, is that "What you are doing speaks so loudly, I can't hear what you are saying!" When your worker's actions differ from his words, it will be his actions that the people among whom he ministers will believe.

The enemies of the cross gave the name "Christian" (little Christ) to the believers in Antioch (see Acts 11:26). It was a dirty word then, but since the followers of the Way were living epistles, known and read by all men, they were easily identifiable. Are we so easy to identify?

A team of college students walked into a remote village in Central America where there were no Christians. Their job was to paint a school building a previous team had built. Because they were excited to share the Lord, the weight of their luggage, paint and equipment seemed light.

As they entered the square, they were met by the village captain. He told them his people had heard all they needed to about this Man Jesus. "We don't want to hear another word you might have to say. Just paint our school building as you said you would. We will watch you. When you have finished, we will let you know if we want your Jesus."

The team knew their outward lives would be living epistles, "the Word written on fleshly tablets of the heart" (2 Corinthians 3:2-3). All they believed about the Word was put to the test in that village.

Those students "walked worthy of the Lord"; when they were ready to leave, ten people including the village captain trusted in Christ as their Savior!

"...*being fruitful unto every good work*" (Colossians 1:10).

There are two considerations for prayer here:

1) That your missionary will be involved in "good work." Unfortunately, there may be thousands of man-hours of effort that aren't even aimed at decisive points of battle.

Your prayers will release the Spirit's guidance in developing a specific strategy "unto every good work" for your missionary. Your prayers of intercession will open his eyes to decisive points of battle.

2) Thus, being involved in good works, you and your worker are interested in seeing "fruit that remains." To birth a child is (to say the least) hard work! Yet, so says the Word, "for the joy that a man is born, the pain is forgotten" (John 16:21). To raise a child in godliness is incomparably more difficult.

To be used of the Spirit to birth a child spiritually and cross-culturally is hard work! To nurture that child to maturity demands the patient endurance of years.

It is true that one sows, another waters, but the Lord gives the increase (see 1 Corinthians 3:6).

"... *and increasing in the knowledge of God*" (Colossians 1:10).

The personal devotional life of your worker is at stake here. On the field there are many factors that can lead to spiritual drought:

1) Your worker may become so busy "working for the

Lord" that there is no time for personal intake. His head can still nod at the appropriate times; his public prayers can still sound almost angelic; his teaching can still be most proper! But the life of the Spirit is gone.

2) Loneliness haunts many cross-cultural workers. More susceptible, of course, are single adults. This can lead to seeking inappropriate relationships, which can lead to spiritual drought.

3) Failure in task takes its toll on some. High American expectations are not met. Discouragement debilitates. This downward spiral of morale is as slippery as grease. At the bottom of the slide are many spiritually depleted field workers. Often these burned-out workers do not realize they should go home. They become an embarrassment to the mission endeavor, a drain on the energies of others who are trying to help them and a dismal blot on the testimony of God's Church in the world!

4) Disillusionment can bring awful frustration, which in turn may lead to spiritual drought. In the mission process there are many tasks that aren't very glamorous—cleaning the grease trap outside the kitchen door, keeping inventory on radio parts, or being reviled by a drunken street-sleeper.

5) One may become discontent with other workers. "Discontent" is putting it mildly! "Radical interpersonal relationship problems" might be more accurate. This is the number one cause of missionary failure. Why? Because Jesus said, "They [the ones your worker has gone out to seek and to save] will know we are His disciples by our love *for one another*" (John 13:35). So here is a major area of attack by the enemy: If he can destroy our unity he will destroy our testimony!

Your prayers and the united intercession of the prayer support team for your cross-cultural worker will put a hedge of protection around him (Ezekiel 22:30), will guard his thoughts (Philippians 4:4-7) and will give him the wisdom of a peacemaker in those tough inter-personal situations (James 3:13-18).

"*...strengthened with all might, according to His glorious power*" (Colossians 1:11).

In Acts 1:4 and 8 Jesus gave clear instruction to His disciples to wait for the power of the Holy Spirit. It's a jungle out there! It is insane to step into cross-cultural outreach ministry without "His glorious power." It is imperative to have a vital, personal, alive, active, growing, dynamic, real relationship with the third Person of the Godhead, the Holy Spirit.

Intercede for your cross-cultural worker that he would be continually being "filled with the Spirit" (Ephesians 5:18). Pray that he will daily "mind the things of the Spirit" (Romans 8). Life and ministry in a second culture (Actually, we *all* walk in an alien world!) hold challenges foreign to your worker but not to the Spirit of God. As you pray, the Spirit of truth will guide him into all truth (John 16:13).

"*...unto all patience and longsuffering with joyfulness*" (Colossians 1:12).

Joe and Sue were ready to leave Brazil. Because they had stayed several months over the two-year visa issued, the federal government in Brasilia had provided them with a letter assuring them all was in order. However, when on departure they presented that letter and their passports (which showed an expired visa) to the state official, he looked at Joe and said, "You are in our country illegally! That will be a $500 fine!" Not having the money, Joe and Sue spent three long days, luggage in tow, trudging from official to official until they were finally permitted to leave.

Missionaries, particularly those in Third World ministries, are more than familiar with bank lines, gas lines, food lines and delays in mail deliveries, material deliveries and baby deliveries! Patience and longsuffering are critical!

But there is another phrase: "with joyfulness." Yes, your worker might in stoicism realize he has no alternative than to wait. But can he brush off the cobwebs of delay with joyfulness? Can the joy of the Lord be his strength as after a two-hour wait in line he steps up to the telegraph clerk's window and is told, "Sorry, we are going on strike right now!"?

Yes, your prayers as vials of sweet incense intercede for him before the Father day and night, meting out to him the measure of grace sufficient for any trial. Prayer is where the action is!

"Giving thanks unto the Father" (Colossians 1:13).

Paul enjoined the Christians in Philippi to "Be anxious for nothing; but in everything by prayer and supplication *with thanksgiving* let your requests be made known to God (Philippians 4:6). A thankful attitude reveals a heart that is right with God.

The pressures of the mission field, however, can produce in your worker something other than a thankful attitude. The difficult living conditions can say, "It's not fair!" The depleting of finances each month can shout, "I need more!" The lack of apparent spiritual response can cry, "You're not worth my time!" The breakdown in health can mull, "I guess God didn't really call me to these people!"

Your prayers can be used to challenge your missionary with Mordecai's words: "Who knows but that for such an hour as this you have been called to the Kingdom?" (Esther 4:14). Your prayers can be used to help your cross-cultural worker identify with Paul: "For I reckon that the sufferings of this present time are not worthy to be compared with the glory which shall be revealed in us" (Romans 8:18). Your prayers can be used to stir the resources that will build in your field worker an attitude of thankfulness: "It is a privilege to be about our Father's business."

In-the-Gap Praying

"And I sought for a man among them that should make up the hedge, and stand in the gap before me for the land, that I should not destroy it: but I found none" (Ezekiel 22:30).

The "gap" mentioned in Ezekiel has been used to express a number of concepts. Prophetically Jesus came to bridge the chasm between God and man. As an appeal to people to go to the mission fields of the world, filling in the "gap" of front-line workers is critical. There are cultural gaps between the missionary and the people group he is trying to reach.

But in the context of Ezekiel, "in the gap" speaks more directly of the role of an intercessor—one who forms a barrier (a hedge) between God (who is speaking) and "the land, that I should not destroy it."

"I looked for a man...." Abraham became that man: "God, will you not spare the city for fifty righteous men? Forty-five? Forty? Thirty? Twenty? Ten? Far be it from Thee to slay the righteous with the wicked.... Shall not the Judge of all the earth do right?" (See Genesis 18.) Those are powerful words for one who had "taken upon himself to speak to the Lord, seeing [he was] but dust and ashes!" He stood in the gap.

"I looked for a man...." Moses became that man: "And Moses besought the face of the Lord his God, and said, 'Lord, why does Your wrath wax hot against *Thy* people?'" Just four verses earlier, in His anger God had called them *Moses'* people! After two more verses of intercession, "the Lord repented of the evil which He thought to do unto *His* people" (Exodus 32:11-14).

Another time Moses even more boldly said: "Yet now, if you will forgive their sin...; and if not, blot me, I pray Thee, out of Your book which You have written!" (Exodus 32:32). Read Deuteronomy chapter nine for a review of the many times Moses stood in the gap for His people. Moses was definitely an "in-the-gap" intercessor!

"I looked for a man...." Aaron became that man (Numbers 16). Nehemiah became that man (Nehemiah). Jesus became that Man (John 17). Paul became that man (Romans 9). Others through the generations of time have become that man, that woman who stood in the gap.

And today Scripture still declares the voice of God—which perhaps says to you, "I looked for *you* to make up the hedge, to stand in the gap!"

A battle is raging for the souls of mankind. In the book of Job, we have been given some insight into the spiritual realm from which this war emanates.

Job had arrived! He was rich. He was famous. He was perfect and upright. He feared God and hated evil. At least this is what the world could see.

But behind the scenes of this visible world is the real world. And Satan saw the hedge complete—not only around Job, but "about his house, and about all that he has on every side" (Job 1:1-10). Two excellent novels, *This Present Darkness* and *Piercing the Darkness* by Frank Peretti, give thought-provoking possibilities to the subtleties of this behind-the-scenes war (see "Resources," page 200).

The "accuser of the brethren" (Revelation 12:10) is "going to and fro in the earth, and is walking up and down in it seeking whom he may devour" (1 Peter 5:8). When he sees the breach in the hedge, the broken-down walls, the secret thoughts of sin, his entrance to the minds and hearts of men is with ease.

And even when that hedge is complete around a man, Satan presents himself before God. It's those "perfect ones" he wants to get. So God, knowing his thoughts, says, "Satan, have you set your heart on my servant, Job?" (Job 1:8).

This is one of the works of the enemy: To set his heart on even the elect, if it were possible (see Matthew 24:24). Jesus said, "Peter, Satan desires to have you to sift you like wheat; but I have prayed for you" (Luke 22:31). Satan and a third of the host of heaven who rebelled against God with him are out to destroy to whatever degree and with whatever diabolical consequences they can connive.

Picture the scene in that heavenly throne room, that secret place you enter boldly to obtain mercy and grace to help in the time of need (Hebrews 4:16). Not only are you and God there as you intercede for the "mercy and grace" your cross-cultural worker needs, but also present is the adversary. The enemy of our souls is telling the truth about our weaknesses or lying through his teeth about us, using any tactic in his fiendish reservoir to break through the hedge, to rush through the gap.

One of the strongest weapons to bind the work of the enemy is the intercessory, effectual, fervent prayer of a committed, united team of believers.

The Prayer Support Team should never be limited in number. A missionary relates: "One morning while trying to watch my son's surgery, I 'decided' to faint! In the process, I sustained a fractured skull and serious brain concussion. For three weeks I lay flat in bed and lived from one pain pill to the next. All the missionaries in the area were praying. But one night my wife got on the ham radio to solicit additional prayer force from the team back home. She contacted our pastor's wife just as she was preparing to go to a church prayer meeting. Following that burst of intercession, I never took another pain pill. I had no more pain. To God be the glory!"

Unbelief is the single most serious factor that breaks down the hedge. God is looking for a team, for a woman, for a man "to make up the hedge, to stand in the gap before Me for the land [in behalf of the people], that I should not destroy it: *but I found none!*" And, in the Ezekiel account, destruction came!

May it not be said of us on that awesome judgement day that He was calling from among us a man, a woman, a prayer support team to stand in the gap, but He found none!

Rather may it be said, "Well done, thou good and faithful servant. Enter thou into the joy of the Lord!" (Matthew 25:21).

Fasting and Prayer

In a trilogy of instruction in what has become known as the Sermon on the Mount, Jesus said, "When you give..., when you pray..., when you fast." He presumes that we *will* fast. He follows each injunction with contrasting instruction: "Don't do it this way; but do do it this way" (Matthew 6:1-18).

Unfortunately, today what most Christians know about fasting and food is *fast food!*

The biblical significance of fasting, however, is so profound throughout the Old and New Testaments that for us to be ignorant of or indifferent toward its place in a Christian's life is equal to spiritual starvation.

"But I'll starve to death!" is exactly the way many Christians respond. Therefore, we need to know the "what, why, when, and how" of fasting.

What is fasting? Both in the secular sense and in the biblical sense, fasting means abstaining from food. A total fast is abstaining from all food and drink (Exodus 34:28). A normal fast allows the intake of drink (Luke 4:2). A limited fast indicates restriction of certain types of foods (Daniel 10:2-3).

Why should we fast? Because Jesus told us to. Isaiah gave clear spiritual and physical purposes for the exercise of fasting:

a) Spiritual: "To loose the bands of wickedness, to undo the heavy burdens, and to let the oppressed go free, and that you break every yoke."

b) Physical: "To deal your bread to the hungry, to bring the poor that are afflicted to your home, to clothe the naked, and to be available to help your own relatives" (Isaiah 58:6-7).

When should we fast? Definitely not when Christ the Bridegroom is around. "But when He is taken up from among them, then they will fast" (Matthew 9:14-15). As we still await the return of the Bridegroom, *now* is the time for fasting!

How should we fast? Definitely "not as the hypocrite who puts on a gloomy face and neglects his appearance in order to be seen fasting by men. Rather, brush your hair and wash your face so that nobody knows that you are fasting. Let it be a secret between you and your Father. For He knows all secrets and will reward you" (Matthew 6:17-18).

Because our bodies are meant to take in food, and there is no spiritual merit in injuring our bodies through fasting, there are other important "do's and don'ts" we must consider as we enter and conclude a time of fasting. The finest work on the subject of fasting is Arthur Wallis' *God's Chosen Fast* (see "Resources," page 200).

When prayer and fasting are practiced in concert, they present a unique and powerful duo. Incorporate the practice of fasting with your prayer support.

Prayer for More Field Workers
Jesus left His outreach headquarters, Capernaum. "He

went about all the cities and villages, teaching in their synagogues and spreading the Gospel of the Kingdom, healing every sickness and disease among the people."

A gruelling itinerary. A heavy schedule. But on one occasion, "when He saw the multitudes, He was moved with compassion on them, because they fainted, and were scattered abroad, as sheep having no shepherd.

"Then He turned to His disciples, and said, 'The harvest truly is plentiful, but the laborers are few: therefore, pray to the Lord of the harvest, that He will send forth laborers into His harvest'" (Matthew 9:35-38).

Having painted a picture of a vast harvest, Jesus shared His means for reaping the harvest: field workers! His harvesters are ordinary human beings who will be obedient to His Great Commission—people who know Him sharing with people who don't.

Jesus tells us to pray to the Father that He will send them forth. There is a crying need for field workers today; this is still a most needed prayer. But be careful when you pray it. Remember that several verses later He sent forth the very men He had instructed to pray!

Prayer for an Entrance of the Gospel

Paul solicited the prayers of the Christians in Colosse with these words: "Include us in your prayer, please, that God may open for us a door for the entrance of the Gospel. Pray that we may talk freely of the mystery of Christ" (Colossians 4:3).

Our prayers should be that the Gospel—the mystery of Christ—no longer remains a mystery to them, but enters through the door of their hearts.

Often a "door" that will open into a culture is a story or tradition in that culture which encourages a receptivity to the Gospel. In missiological circles these are called "redemptive analogies."

For example, missionary Bruce Olson found that the

Motilone Indians of the jungles of Colombia had a ceremony in which they cried for a god to come out of a hole dug in the ground. Olson used this tradition as a bridge to tell the Motilone of the resurrected Christ—Who came out of His tomb, a "hole in the ground"!

Two of the best books on this subject are, *Eternity in Their Hearts* by Don Richardson, and *The Discovery of Genesis* by C.H. Kang and Ethel R. Nelson (see "Resources," page 200).

So pray for opening doors as your field workers research to discover redemptive analogies for the people among whom they labor.

Prayer to Bind the Strong Man
As Paul told the Christians in Corinth that he would stay in Ephesus until Pentecost, he said, "For a great and effectual door has opened unto me, *and there are many adversaries*" (1 Corinthians 16:9).

Behind every open door of opportunity, there are enemies of the cross—always one with a foot stuck out to trip up those who would walk through. Sometimes the enemy is even able to use the actions of other believers to thwart plans!

There is a time to resist the devil (James 4:7). There is a time to cast out devils (Mark 16:17). There is a time to bind the works of the enemy, to bind the "strong man" himself (Matthew 18:18; Mark 3:27). And there is a time to inhibit his activity and pseudo-authority in the affairs of men (1 John 3:8).

This takes bold men and women praying bold prayers, for the enemy does not like being exposed for the fraud he is.

Prayer for His Kingdom to Come
Jesus said it so simply: "When you pray, say... 'Thy Kingdom come'" (Luke 11:2). Pray for the people into

whose lives the Kingdom has not yet come.

More than two billion individuals in nearly 12,000 distinct people groups are today without a solid Gospel witness, many with no knowledge of even the *name* of Jesus Christ. More than 55,000 die every day without a chance to respond to the message of salvation in Christ.

And we are not talking only about those who live in deep, dark jungles. An evangelist was sitting with his team at the breakfast table of a hotel restaurant in Singapore, a city/nation that enjoys a higher standard of living than the United States and is home to thousands of believers. The group had their Bibles out, and the waitress asked them what that Book was. "The Bible," they told her. Her response: "What is a Bible?" She had never heard of such a Book!

Pray for fallow ground to be broken up (Jeremiah 4:3). Pray for the seed to fall on fertile soil (Matthew 13:3-9). Pray that the waterers will neither drench nor parch the seedling. Pray that the cultivators will not mar the plant by misusing their tools. Pray that the Lord of the Harvest will give the increase (1 Corinthians 3:6).

What a privilege that He allows us to participate in His Plan of the Ages by coming boldly before Him, interceding on behalf of the lost of the world as well as for the workers who have gone out to the fields of the world. If God be for us, who can be against us? What an unequal contest it seems!

It is prayer that links the missionary enterprise to the irresistible power of God. Prayer is the fulcrum on which the battle turns. The mightiest weapon we can use is the weapon of prayer—potent, powerful, prevailing prayer, the prayer of faith against which the adversary has no effective counterweapon.

Pray without ceasing.

Case Study in Prayer Support

How does the Core Group we have been following handle prayer support?

Our prayer support for Lou and Sandy is much harder to talk about than the other areas of support. For example, in regards to financial support, we can discuss how we raised monthly support and then have the concrete evidence every month when the checks come into the church office that the people are following through with their commitment.

But prayer support is a little more difficult. At best we can say how we've tried to encourage people to pray, and how we pray that they are following through with their commitment.

One element of prayer support is an awareness of needs. Lou and Sandy's needs are made known in several ways:

1) Everyone committed to support them in prayer is encouraged to have one clock in their house set to Filipino time (16 hours ahead). When we wake up at 6 a.m. and realize that it is 10 p.m. the *next day* in the Philippines, it can prompt us to pray with an increased awareness—perhaps for a good night's sleep!

2) Lou and Sandy have a monthly newsletter they mail out to supporters with a specific section summarizing their prayer needs. This portion of the letter can be cut out, highlighted and stuck to the refrigerator with the photo magnet of Lou and Sandy that each supporter received in their initial packet.

3) Two prayer chains have been formed. A prayer chain is simply a list of names and phone numbers. As a prayer request is made known via letter, phone call or fax, the person at the top of the list is notified. He phones the next person on the list who then relays the message to the next person and so

on until all are made aware of the need.

Two prayer chains were developed for this reason: It was felt that there may be times when a need would arise that was of such a personal nature that it might be best if only the Core Group and a few others determined by Lou and Sandy would know about it in detail. The second prayer chain would receive that prayer request in more general terms. Other requests may be given to both groups.

Another element of prayer support is to be able to intercede as led by the Holy Spirit without even knowing the needs. Or, perhaps, the information we receive indicating their needs aren't really the needs at all! It is necessary for us then, by the Spirit, to perceive the real needs as we get together in intercession for Lou and Sandy and the people among whom they're ministering. We're always trying to expand our prayer so we include the people group; Lou and Sandy will be coming home one day, and it seems only reasonable we would develop hearts for the needs of those people now so we can keep praying for God's activity among them for years to come.

One way we are attempting to increase the efficacy of our prayers was expressed in a recent mailing we sent out to all prayer supporters. In it we asked for volunteers to make a weekly commitment to fast and pray for one hour. We suggested a dinner fast (actually starting right after lunch) with a prayer time following in the evening. We also stated that if they felt led to commit to a longer fast or even a partial fast, that was certainly between them and the Lord. We asked them to make this a four-month commitment and to complete an enclosed form detailing what day they had chosen to fast. This has been on a strictly voluntary basis. The results in terms of commitment will ultimately be seen in a new release of the Lord's power in Lou and Sandy as they go about their work.

There is so much to learn in this area of support. May the Lord grant us ever willing hearts to grow in prayer and may we be ever submissive to get down on our knees and be about our Father's business through prayer.

Prayer is truly a powerful weapon to be used in the spiritual conflicts encountered in cross-cultural ministry. Yet, again, there are other aspects of your worker's life that must be considered. He as a cultural being will want you to keep in touch with him through *communication* support.

(In addition to the individual study below, see the **Group Leader's Guide** for session five beginning on page 191.)

For Your Personal Involvement

• Keep a record for one week of the prayers you pray. Is there a good mixture of praise, personal petition, intercession and thanksgiving?

• Study the prayers of several Bible characters. (Be sure to include the publican!) Or read through all the prayers of one person. Identify if each is a prayer of thanksgiving, praise, personal petition or intercession. Become familiar with the way the prayer sounds. Compare (or contrast) them with your style of praying.

• Locate, read and study the nineteen recorded prayers of Jesus.

• Begin or become part of a missions prayer group where you can learn to participate in the power of united prayer.

• Read Arthur Wallis' book *God's Chosen Fast.*

Action Steps

By the time you have read Chapter Five, completed the *For Your Personal Involvement* section and participated in a discussion group, you should...

• More closely pray the prayers of the Bible. Be on guard against the ever-popular "gimmie" prayers.

• Be able to decide if prayer support is a commitment you can make to your missionary. If you can, write to him, letting him know of that commitment and of your desire to be kept informed of his prayer needs.

• Practice the Christian discipline of fasting.

• Pray without ceasing!

• Multiply yourself. Actively look for others in your circle of relationships who have or who might develop a heart for prayer.

Chapter Six Communication Support

"Lord willing, I plan to send Timothy to you soon so that I may be comforted when I know how you are doing."

Philippians 3:19

"I had zilch knowledge of missions and no preparation, whatsoever! I knew God wanted me to go to Paris, but even that was only confirmed in my heart after I arrived there. My home church's 'policy' was to lay hands on you, say a prayer and wave, 'Goodbye!' My home fellowship group said they would write to me and pray for me. I wrote to them faithfully about every five weeks. I received one letter from them the first year and one the second!

"Lack of communication further hit me when I arrived. I was to work with another missionary from my church who was helping equip lay leaders in a new church near the Latin Quarter. When I got there, I found out that he had moved to another city!

"A local national church took me in. I began learning servanthood in a cross-cultural setting. Sweeping, cleaning toilets, dusting, sorting clothes and running errands were my first assignments. After I regained my ability in the language, I began teaching in their day school for children.

"Lack of communication also hit my pocketbook! I arrived in Paris with $15 and a promise of a temporary place to stay. (Remember, I had had no training.) I was never taught how to raise financial support. I had not communicated my needs before I left, nor in my letters once I was gone. I thought it was 'bad' to talk about money. Now I know I should give full information and allow others to share in His ministry that way.

"I got a small check from a friend through my church the first month. Well into the second month I called my brother to call my church to see if any money had come in for me and if they had mailed it. Only $45 had come in and it had been mailed, returned for postage, and mailed again! Anyway, I moved ten times that first year because I had to live wherever I could without paying rent.

"By then I had come to accept it: This is missionary life—until I met Bill and Louise. It began when they offered to help me financially. I felt bad because their church was supporting *them* and they were using some of it to help me. Yet, my church was doing nothing to help me.

"As I got to know them better, I saw that not only were their finances in order, but a whole communication network was in place. Regular mail. Frequent 'care' packages. Phone calls of friendship (not of desperation, like mine).

"But I really saw how it *could* be when their church's cross-cultural coordinator, John, came to visit them. It was just a one-day visit as he was in Europe on other business, but I saw real caring. He had prepared a special Bible study that he said the Lord had given him just for them. He brought a computer banner saying, "We really do miss you!" It had personal notes scribbled all over it. There were special goodies for their children.

"I came to realize that to the extent the communication, prayer and financial support was strong from their sending church—to that extent their ministry was strong. John said I could call on them any time there was a need. He didn't know the extent of my hurting. (Or did he?) I received a form letter once a year from my church telling me what *they* were doing (Yes, I was even listed as one of their 'accomplishments'!), but they never once asked me how *I* was doing! I had a lot of anger and hurt inside towards my church before coming back because I felt they didn't care.

"After two years I did come home. And I realized the misunderstanding was as much a lack of my communication as theirs. I was open with my home fellowship. I learned that *they* thought the church was supporting me and *I* thought they knew of my condition and need! We just hadn't communicated!

"I got some good training in communication skills. I learned to be open in sharing my needs for communication as well as for prayer, finances and the other areas of support.

"I am back in Paris, now. No, I don't expect a visit from anyone from my church with banners and goodies. But I do have an established foundation of a strong and growing support team from my home fellowship and other individuals in my church and family. And we're communicating! May God be praised!"

It is hard to imagine the importance of communication from home until you have "been there." When a person or family arrives on the field to establish their new routine, real loneliness can set in—a feeling of isolation, of being out of it. A new missionary can feel, "They have forgotten me!" "They aren't writing" might be interpreted: "They don't care! I'm out of their sight—and therefore out of their mind! And I am going out of mine!"

One family recently returned to Israel, this time with two children. The wife recalls, "The first two weeks I was filled with guilt for doing this to my children. I had taken them away from the grandparents who cherish them and whom they adore. I had taken them away from *Sesame Street,* a wonderful library, swimming lessons and food they love. I had taken them away from carpeted floors to fall on, trashless parks with grass instead of broken glass, cool weather, Sunday school—from friends, drinkable water that doesn't make them sick, a familiar doctor I can trust, a car instead of a bus or having to walk in the blazing sun and a mommy with lots of energy, patience and joy!

"Well," she says, "a phone call from Amy back in my home town revealed that she had felt the same way when she first went to Greece. I still wasn't completely convinced that I was doing the best for my boys; but if Amy got through it—and her kids are great...and I do trust God Who is my Father and theirs, Who only wants the best for us....

"After the call, I began to think, 'To tell the truth, David and Daniel seem to be adapting more quickly than I am!' Two-year-old David even reminded me of a Hebrew word that I couldn't think of the other day. And Daniel has learned how to fall on these hard floors without getting a big bump on his head.

The missionary concludes, "Even my mother is handling this well. She recently encouraged me in a letter: 'God wants you there, Mary. Your kids could get sick here, too. C'mon, toughen up!' It seems every time we get discouraged, some bit of communication comes through to *encourage* us!"

Communicating Through Letters

Though Paul, the most prolific New Testament writer, did not have access to the telephone, postal system, fax machines or a computer electronic bulletin board, he knew the importance of personal communication. His letters are shot through with bits of personal comments:

- Requests for his support team to "bring his cloak when they come to him and especially the parchments" (2 Timothy 4:13).

- An earnest appeal to "prepare your guest room for me" (Philemon 22).

- In his powerful letter to the Christians in Rome—that great treatise on grace—he devotes almost all of chapter 16 to personal messages. No less than 41 people are specifically mentioned. Tertius, who has been writing the Roman letter for Paul, might have gotten so excited about all this exchange of greetings that he leaned over and nudged Paul: "Paul, may I say 'Hi,' too?" Verse 22 reads, "I, Tertius, send my Christian greetings also!"

James personalized his short letter 17 times by referring to the dispersed tribes as "my brothers." John, when writing to his friend Gaius and again to "the elect lady," found it difficult to put into words all he wanted to say (2 John 12; 3 John 13). Yet in writing his Gospel he wanted a scroll the size of the whole world to write everything on his heart (John 21:25). Luke, for the sake of his friend Theophilus, "searched out diligently...from the highest to the minutest detail," to set in order the record of the Gospel of Christ and the Acts of the Apostles (Luke 1:1-4).

Peter and Paul found it not burdensome to remind their readers again and again of especially important things (2 Peter 1:12; Philippians 3:1). Jude, as he sat to write his brief letter, intended to make it a light, happy rejoicing in their common salvation. But as he took pen in hand, the Spirit of God compelled him to exhort them to "earnestly contend for the faith" (Jude 3).

Whether on papyrus, parchment, linen or recycled paper, letter writing is the easiest, most common way of keeping in touch; it is the mainstay of communication.

What to Communicate

The content of your communication is vital. Say things that really matter. Not just "How are you? I am fine. Went to the store today. Had meatloaf for dinner." (Of course, they'll read *anything* from home! But....)

Rather, share your thoughts and feelings—what is really going on in your life. How is God working in you? Be realistic and honest but don't use them as your counselor. Remember, you are *their* support.

Get involved in their lives on the field as much as you can. Express interest in the concerns of their hearts. Ask questions about their lives there and respond to what they have said in their previous letters to you. This is especially encouraging because it shows that you really read their letters and are interested enough for some follow-up conversation about it.

One sending team member says, "My wife and I are on the communication support team of over 80 missionaries. We receive 40 to 50 letters every month. When I read their letters, I have a pen in hand to jot down notes or circle specific thoughts I want to respond to. This is the only way we can answer that many letters! And it will work for you, as well."

Share how God is leading you to pray for them. Ask for their specific and personal prayer requests and updates on things about which you previously prayed.

Share a particularly meaningful sermon you just heard, church news or news about a mutual friend— edifying news, of course!

When communicating with missionaries serving in restricted-access countries where their ministry may be considered illegal, be sure to check with your church or mission agency for guidelines when writing about Christian matters and ministries.

Don't forget to have your kids write to the children in your missionary family. This is good training for them to become aware of and involved in missions! Also, grand-mas and grandpas, aunts and uncles: Keep in contact with your grandkids, nieces and nephews. They need to hear from you.

Let's look back at the biblical writers referred to for some patterns for you to follow in your letters to your cross-cultural workers:

Paul to the Romans: Use names to make the stories real. Instead of, "The whole church says 'Hi'!" give the names of specific people they know who said "Hi."

James to the dispersed tribes: Make it a friendly letter, personalized with terms of endearment. Even though (or maybe, because) James had some tough things to say, he reminded them of the personal relationship uniting them. "Though miles separate us, we are still friends; you are not forgotten" is the feeling communicated when you make the letter personal.

John to Gaius and the "elect lady": The time will come when it is tough to sit down and write. You don't know what to say or how to say it. Probably the single greatest hindrance to letter writing is waiting for a big block of time. Don't wait—it will probably never come!

It is not so important to be organized or have nice paper or be able to write pages and pages. What is important is to just do it! Jot down a thought or two on any piece of paper. A day or so later when you have another thought, write it down! When you have accumulated a "letter's worth," mail it! Of course, it would help to at least number the pieces of paper!

A missionary recalls, "One of my favorite letters came on John F. Kennedy Airport tissue paper, written while a support team friend was waiting for an international flight! The novelty of it assured me of the instant inspiration of the words written!"

John to readers of his Gospel: Don't feel that you have to write every word of every conversation of every friend of theirs for every day they are gone! Allow the Spirit to guide you to share those incidents and stories that would be uplifting, informative and motivating.

How you say things also has its impact. Consider the following contrast:

"Well, Jerry has taken your place and is doing such a great job with your home fellowship group that everything is just fine without you" vs. "Wow! God's timing is so perfect. Just as He called you to Alma Ata, He has raised up Jerry to continue the good work you were doing with the home fellowship group."

Luke to Theophilus: Be accurate in your reporting to your friends. Distance and time and cultures already have their way of distorting facts. Memory blurs. You want to communicate a true report of what's going on among the people back home.

Peter and Paul to readers of their epistles: Sometimes with Peter and Paul you will say, "I do not tire of reminding you again and again to be diligent in your personal devotion to God." Don't be afraid to encourage and encourage with the same themes and reminders often—as the Spirit directs you.

Jude to those called of God: As you get in the habit of regular letter writing, you will begin anticipating what you want to say. As you listen to the words of a new song on the radio, you will realize how that would minister to your friend. You jot them down. As you return to a familiar recreation site or a favorite restaurant, a pleasant memory inspires you to relate an incident. So you sit down to write, just wanting to rejoice about the good things of life. But then don't be surprised if there is also a stirring in your soul as the Holy Spirit says, "I have an important message for you to share. Warn him to be on his guard for 'ungodly men who are bent on thwarting the grace of God'" (Jude 4).

Other Ways of Communicating

This need for contact with "home" is nothing new. You remember the story of David, away from his home in Bethlehem. In the heat of battle, he longed for a drink of water from his favorite well over by the city gate (2 Samuel 23:15). His son, Solomon, said, "As cold water to a thirsty soul, so is good news from a far land" (Proverbs 25:25). The need for news from back home isn't new at all, but our world has certainly advanced in its methods of communication.

The telephone, for example, lets you call anywhere in the world for under $10! You wouldn't use this method as regularly as a letter, but even just once can be a really special treat. You can be led by the Spirit to call at a needy time in your missionary's life.

A communicating sender says, "One time I was reading a letter from our cross-cultural worker. It wasn't so much what the letter said (since it had been written two weeks before) as it was the Spirit quickening my mind to understand her present need. I checked the time. It should be about 7 a.m. in Israel. She should still be at home. I dialed. On the second ring, I heard her voice. And we talked for a few minutes. What did we say? I don't remember! But she still talks about that phone call that came at just the right time!"

Faxed messages and telexes can communicate with your cross-cultural worker who may have access to a fax or telex machine. The work of communicating is still there. But these devices make the exchange of ideas more rapid and convenient.

Ham radio is an exciting communication channel. If your worker is in a more remote part of the world, he may know a ham radio operator. If so, have him give you the call letters and the times he is usually on the air. Then find an operator in your area. These people are usually happy to set up a "phone patch" for you to talk with your friend—often free! Around the world!

Communicate through photos. Enclose a photo now and then with your letter. A missionary recalls, "When we were on the field, we had a wall of pictures of friends and family. After all, it was the only place we saw their smiling faces. It was a lingering point for memories and prayer."

One of the missionary's sending team adds, "We have our own wall of cork arranged as the continents of the world. Over a hundred pictures (updated as they send new ones) place our missionary friends in their respective countries. It is for us, too, a location for prayer and memories in our house."

Videotaping is inexpensive and offers endless communication possibilities. Videotape your home fellowship meeting. Update your worker with a traveling tour of what's going on in your town. Tape a family gathering. Interview people he knows as they come out of church, and introduce him to the new comers. Send tapes of special programs, ceremonies and sermons.

Have a video recorder at your next potluck dinner. Conduct a survey of any ridiculous thing, such as: "In your opinion, if a Hotentot tot is taught to talk 'ere the tot can totter, ought the Hotentot tot be taught to say aught or not, or what ought to be taught her?" If that isn't enough for a few laughs for your missionary family, you might want to give them the second verse: "If, to hoot and to toot be taught to a Hotentot tot by a Hotentot tutor, ought the Hotentot tutor get hot if the Hotentot tot hoots and toots at the Hotentot tutor?"

There are excellent Christian videos for kids. What you send may be the only viewing your workers' children can watch since in many countries television is far more explicit than in North America. There are, of course, good entertaining and training videos for adults, as well.

One organization has dedicated itself to providing cassettes, compact discs and video selections for missionaries at greatly reduced prices. The catalog is called *For Missionaries Only* from Mount Carmel, PO Box 243, Leavenworth WA 98826 USA (1-800-272-2442).

Be sure to check with your missionary for the type of videos his tape player uses; different operating systems for video are used in different countries.

Send audiotape letters. Just begin talking into the cassette recorder as if you are talking to your friend in person. It is hard at first because there is no feedback. But that barrier of one-way communication can be overcome. And it is refreshing to hear each other's voices as you develop this method of sharing. They can record over the same tape in their response to you.

Send a group audiotape made at a family gathering or an impromptu interview with people as they come out of church: "Hey, in 20 words or less, what do you want to say to ——?" (Name your missionary.) Have the "roving mike" catch their first words! Let your field worker rejoin the home fellowship meeting by recording services and get-togethers. Fill their ears with the sounds of the kids choir or crickets chirping and frogs croaking or the freeway—if that's what they miss.

A "care" package is a great idea. Of course, check first with the post office and with your missionary or agency on what may be sent. Find out how to label packages properly. It is amazing what you can put even in a letter envelope, thus making the shipping easier. Determine what your shipping costs plus their duty costs will be; otherwise you might send a package that costs double or triple what it is worth.

There are many items that will communicate your love: new books, music tapes, Bible study tapes. One cross-cultural worker one mentioned that he really enjoys the Sunday sports section of his local newspaper. A loyal friend now mails it to him every week! Sometimes even the little things that seem like nothing to us—a package of salad dressing mix or chili powder—are a delightful surprise if your missionaries live where those items are not available.

But don't be surprised if their tastes have changed. Ask them what their needs and their wants are now. No matter how mundane the request, if it will minister to them, send it!

Personal visits, of course, are the ultimate in communication. How Paul longed to see his support team. And he thanked them profusely when they sent a representative to minister to his needs (see Philippians 4:15-18, for example).

One church takes a tour to Israel each year. Their missionaries in Greece and Turkey have the opportunity every other year to spend this time with their friends from back home—in Israel! The church pays the missionaries' fares to come from their place of ministry to Israel for these ten days of fellowship and vacation.

The missions pastor of one church regularly travels to the locations of the church's missionaries to put "new heart" in them and to encourage them in the Lord.

Even if you or one from your fellowship cannot make the visit, if you know of someone going to your worker's location or nearby, you can encourage that traveler to visit your missionary, to hand-carry a message or package of love and concern. On the other hand, if your worker lives in a major crossroads of world travelers, you might need to "protect" him from being a perpetual host and tour guide!

Communication support is caring and expressing it; caring *is* communication!

A Case Study in Communication Support
Lou and Sandy's support team makes a special effort to communicate with them:

Since my husband and I moved into the duplex that Lou and Sandy moved out of, we take care of their mail. Most people send personal mail directly to the Philippines, so we basically collect Lou's magazines, newsletters and other third class mail and a few personal letters that may not be mailed directly to them. We mail all of this in a manila envelope once or twice a month, depending on the accumulation. Bank statements, tax papers, bills and other legal papers we hand over to Tim, who is in charge of Logistics Support.

We also send the Sunday sermon tape in that envelope. Often we include an interesting front page of our local newspaper or Lou's favorite comics! Lou keeps asking us about developments in world affairs. We try to keep him aware of what's going on. He recently got a shortwave radio, though, so his requests in this area have slowed down.

We have also sent care packages. We try to send special treats for each of them—things that they cannot buy where they live. In each one we include a treat or gift for their host family or the national staff with whom they work.

Because communication is two-way, on one Sunday each month we put up a Philippines Mission table. There is an attractive display with updated information about Lou and Sandy and the mission with which they work. At this table we hand out pre-addressed aerograms to people who will write that month to Lou and Sandy.

Apparently there has been no lack of letter communication. In one six-week period, they reported, they had gone only three days without at least one letter, and one day they had received seven!

One month Lou (who is interested in statistical analysis) kept tract of the postmarks on the mail they received. (That, in itself, is telling us they are getting a good amount of mail!)

Lou reported, "In checking the postmarks from our supporters to see how long it took for the mail to get to us, we noticed a bell curve based on the arrival of our prayer letter to them. Forty-seven per cent of our communication support team sent their letters to us within a week of their receiving our letter! It pays to write *and* to personalize our letters!"

The ultimate in communication support was afforded Lou and Sandy last summer. Our mission pastor and his family took part of their vacation to visit them in the Philippines. We sent our love along with them in a hundred tangible ways. And they returned our love with thankful hearts.

"Reach out and touch someone," the Bell telephone system used to say. You can still do it through soul-satisfying communication support. But the full circle of supporting your missionary is completed as you receive him back home through *re-entry* support.

(In addition to the individual study below, see the **Group Leader's Guide** for session six beginning on page 193.)

For Your Personal Involvement

* Read one of Paul's letters and highlight all references to personal messages and comments. You may be surprised how much of his letters dealt with personal communication, logistics and the desire to just relate his friendship.

* Select one of the other letter-writers in the Bible. Identify what kinds of "homey" things he talked about.

* Check with the mission groups of other churches to discover what specific ideas they use in their communication support.

* Talk with your (or other) missionaries who are on furlough. Find out from them the kinds of communication support they receive, which are appreciated most and why.

* Review the different methods of communication suggested in this chapter. Which are you particularly interested in? Do you have the necessary equipment for that or those methods?

Action Steps

By the time you have read Chapter Six, completed the *For Your Personal Involvement* section and participated in a discussion group, you should...

* Be able to decide if this is the area of support the Lord is directing you into. If so, get out pen and paper now! Write to that missionary God has put on your heart and mail it *today!*

* Prepare a form for father, mother, and children to be completed before they go, telling of their needs and wants. Be sure to include a place for their birthdays and anniversaries, types of books they like, music or study tapes they enjoy. If your missionaries are already on the

field, mail the form to them. When they return it, be sure to follow through regularly with at least some of their requests.

• If your worker is overseas, find out what types of things survive through the mail and what things to avoid sending. Determine costs of packages of various weights and the approximate time it takes between sending and receiving a package.

• Multiply yourself. Actively share what you are doing and look for others who might get involved.

"And they abode a long time with the disciples there."
Acts 14:28

"My father was a career missionary. My brothers and sisters and I were born on the mission field. This was our life. Dad diligently directed a theological seminary for the whole western region of the country. Mother stood faithfully by his side. Our education was as much enhanced by watching their lives as it was by the lessons in our classrooms.

"Through the years they had weathered any number of storms that assail missionaries. Each brought them to a more determined level of commitment to our Lord and to the cause of training national leadership.

"Tensions between national Christians and missionary leadership were frequent. But my dad was a peacemaker. He could walk that delicate line of cultural sensitivity. Lack of funds became so common that we all knew when to 'tighten our belts.' Discouragement over 'promising' national students who turned their backs on Christian service only toughened Dad's resolve to pour his life into others.

"But probably the most trying experience Dad and Mom faced was his arrest and uncertain life and death outcome during a military coup. With all the dramatics of a war movie, soldiers barged into our house and took Dad captive. They were sure he had 'secret contacts with the enemies of the people.'

"The coup failed. After three weeks Dad was released and resumed his work at the seminary.

"We kids are grown now. Several of us are married and back on the mission field ourselves.

"Last summer Dad called us all together for a family meeting. By the curtness of the invitation and the insistence on our being there, we could tell *something* was wrong. In a thousand years we would have never dreamed of what would take place. The meeting was short and to the point. In essence: 'Children, it is important for you to know that I am divorcing your mother. I plan to marry Sue.' Sue is younger than I am! His parting words were, 'And furthermore, I'm not even sure there is a God!'"

In the secular world they are saying it: Re-entry is often the hardest part of an overseas experience and it should not be ignored. There are unexpected problems in returning home. Family members who have lived in another culture need to learn how to overcome the difficulties of today's workplace, community and school environments.

In the Christian community they are saying it: Up to 50% of first-time missionaries return home early or don't return for a second term. These wounded people need to identify and process the hurt and anger of failure—to begin to build up their lives again, growing toward mental and spiritual wholeness.

In missions seminars they are saying it: One leader emphasized, "I have not taught one seminar about the drastic need for re-entry help without some missionary coming to me, saying, 'I thought I was weird. I couldn't tell anyone about my feelings. Thank you for letting me know that it is okay to feel a little uncomfortable in coming home.'

"Recently, just as I finished the re-entry session of a seminar, a woman in the front began sobbing, then uncontrollably weeping. Finally, through her tears, she wailed, 'I have been home from Indonesia for three months. Everything you just talked about—I am experiencing. Please help me!'"

The Situation Of Re-entry

There is an initial *shock* in returning home. Old buildings have been torn down; new ones have taken their place. A favorite park is now a freeway interchange. Grandma's rocking chair is empty. Your cross-cultural worker probably heard about all of these things as they happened. But now that he is home and sees them for himself, he's jolted. As with an electric shock, though, these factors are gradually absorbed and accepted.

The *stress* of coming home is another issue. There is a mental stretching as new ideas and ideals are incorporated into the old—which isn't old anymore since it also is new and strangely different.

There is a spiritual duress caused by the continual memory of the needs of a world lost in sin and what we are or *aren't* doing about those needs.

There is a physical taffy-pull as well-meaning people gorge their newly returned missionary with rich American non-food foods. "You're so skinny; have some more!"

There are odd emotions, as perhaps your missionary tries to justify the new $1,000 wardrobe of clothes that has just been graciously given him. Days before he left the field, his national partner had refused to receive a shirt from him with the words, "I have one to wear while I wash the other. A third one would just be wasted!"

Yes, the home scene with its people, places, and things—all that *you* represent—has changed. But more dramatically, your missionary friend has changed—socially, emotionally, mentally, physically and most of all spiritually. And because these changes happened to each of you so gradually, you yourselves are only slightly aware of them. But as you meet, the changes in each other appear drastic!

Needless to say, the longer your cross-cultural worker has been away, the more pronounced will be the culture stress in coming home.

But even short assignments can produce dramatically bold changes. The Apostle Paul's entire life was changed in the span of just a few minutes on the Damascus road!

In many situations of world need today, God can instantly open your missionary's eyes to crying needs for ministry. Short-term mission trainers report, "For simple exposure to another culture, we have taken people across the border into Mexico and watched God break their hearts with compassion for the lost and needy of this world in just one afternoon."

There is another factor to consider in re-entry support: denial. Some workers may prepare to return home denying that they will face any stress upon re-entry. Some steel themselves with the attitude that "it won't—it can't happen to me."

Denial can be suicide—emotional, spiritual, mental. And even literal, physical suicide has been the result of some missionaries' shock and stress in re-entry. Your returning missionary may think, "Look how easy it was for me to adjust to my new culture on the field. What's the big deal? I'm just going home!"

Look at some possible blind spots in that statement:

1) The adaptation probably wasn't as easy as he now remembers it;

2) The months (maybe years) of anticipation before going gave him time to prepare for the adjustments;

3) The nationals of the host culture may have been accustomed to Americans and therefore knew how to help him adapt. In many cultures the people are very gentle, non-demanding and forgiving of missionaries.

None of those factors will cushion his re-entry as he comes home. Perhaps his unaware friends back home are echoing the same words: "What's the big deal? He's just coming home!" Because many of them have not ventured beyond the comfort zones of their own world, they have no idea of what a missionary goes through in living and ministering in a second culture. Many supporters feel coming home is basically a non-issue.

Awareness of the factors of re-entry can prepare you to become a strongly supportive friend in the "coming back home" process.

The Challenge Of Re-entry
As a re-entry support person, it is necessary for you to keep your eyes and ears open for signs of culture stress in reverse. The returning field worker is the one least prepared to handle the situation. He knows something's not right! The loneliness, the disappointment and letdown, feelings of isolation and not belonging here, the dizzying speeds of everything may find him silently crying, "Slow down! Slow down!" But it doesn't slow down.

You must take the initiative. You must be the "intensive care unit" for your missionary's re-entry.

He will face challenges of re-entry in any one or more of the following areas:

1) Professionally
After the adventure of an overseas experience, going back to his old job could be very boring. Equally perplexing could be the "big-fish-in-a-little-pond" syndrome. Upon return, he suddenly becomes a small-to-

medium-sized-fish in a much bigger pond! He may lament, "The light of my testimony looked so much brighter out there where it was dark!" Possibly he will sense an under-utilization of the skills and experiences he gained on the field. Or he may feel the loss of some degree of independence as he is now under the more watchful eye of his employer. Or the feeling of being in the old rat race may begin to haunt him.

In some areas of work, a year or two away may find the old job obsolete. One woman working in computers realized this during her field training before she went as a short-termer to the field. Helping her through that stress before she left for the field made re-entry easier for her later. In fact, when she returned, she said, "I'm not going back into computers. I am working at a nursing home. I see this as a ministry now, and the medical training I'm getting will really open up new opportunities for me to go again where laborers are needed."

2) Materially-Financially

The America your worker is coming back to is generally much more expensive. That doesn't mean that a loaf of bread necessarily costs more. It does mean that Americans spend more money on *things* than do the people of the culture from which he is returning.

When your cross-cultural workers return to this, it may cause stress! When they see a teenager go to a full closet of clothes and cry, "I don't have anything to wear!" they remember the hours they labored over how to ask "the people back home" for a few extra dollars to feed and clothe the neighborhood kids.

One recently returned missionary said, "The wealth of this country is very difficult to handle; the wealth of the church is even more difficult for me to deal with."

Another missionary said, "It happened to my wife this way: A few months after our return from Mozambique, she was leisurely walking the aisles of a super-market, choosing this and wisely picking that off the shelves. All of a sudden, a feeling of being overwhelmed consumed her. She began thinking, 'There are too many choices. I have to get out of here!' She left her half-full cart right in the aisle, went to the car and drove home!"

Another recalled, "In Brazil, due to our various economic and living conditions, *personal ownership* took a back seat in our minds. Upon our arrival home, I began working with a fellow who was using a new Bic felt point pen. They had not been on the market when we left. He let me use it. I commented to him how I enjoyed the feel of it and how good the writing looked.

"The next day he *gave* me one. 'Here, this is yours!' For several days, I would pause and just look at that 59¢ treasure. 'It's mine! It's really mine!' I would muse to myself."

"Ridiculous!" you might say. Yes, but this is the very level on which culture stress in reverse occurs.

Comparative wealth can begin the stress even before your missionaries leave the field. And children are susceptible as well as adults: Bill and Alice were house parents in a children's home for Wycliffe Bible Translators in the northern Philippines. Their son William had had an opportunity to spend a week in a tribal village.

Sometime after his return to the Wycliffe Center, Alice saw William looking into his clothes closet. He was crying. Knowing her own concern for how little they had compared to their lifestyle back in the States, she went to console him. After several attempts at resisting her comfort, he said, "No, Mom. I feel sad that I have *so much* in comparison to my new friends in the tribe."

3) Culturally
New beliefs, values, attitudes and behaviors have become a part of your returning worker. Perhaps he has

adjusted to a culture with a slower pace, a more relaxed atmosphere, an emphasis on people and relationships, zestier foods, a noon-hour siesta....

The cultural differences that your returning missionary may try to hold onto are innumerable. When schedules and attitudes of people here at home now don't allow for them, he feels irritation and *stress!*

One major expectation of most returnees is that people will be interested in their experiences: "We had been invited to their house for the evening," one returning missionary wrote. "We assumed it was to be able to share the excitement of our missionary venture. After a delicious meal during which we were able to insert a few comments, we were ushered into the family room. 'Now is our opportunity,' I thought. But as our host turned on the TV, he said, 'I was sure you would enjoy watching the NFL playoffs on our new 29-inch screen!' I was absolutely devastated!"

What a different story is told of the Antioch church welcoming home their travel-weary pioneer missionaries: "From there they sailed back to Antioch where they had first been commended to the grace of God for the task which they had now completed. When they arrived there, they called the whole church together and rehearsed before them *all* that God had done with them, and how He had opened the door of faith to the Gentiles" (Acts 14:26-27).

4) Socially

Many people place an "unholy" halo about a missionary. He is held aloof as if he is right next to God.

"How can we relate with someone who has been a missionary?" they wonder. "What would we talk about?"

Or some may fear that the missionary is contagious! "If I have them over for dinner, will my kids come down with some kind of exotic diseases?" Worse! "Their enthusiasm for missions might rub off on me!"

It might seem to returning missionaries that everyone is hurrying here and there. After spending some time here, one perceptive international observed: "In America, everyone has a watch, but no one has any time. In our country, few have watches, but everybody has time!"

Compared to much of the rest of the world, life in the United States is extremely busy. When your missionary went to the field, his old friends closed the gap that was created in their lives by his departure. Social ties may have been broken with time. Former friends' children have made new friends. Once-dear families may have moved away.

If communication between the missionary and his home church has not been good or if it is a particularly large church, he may not have even been missed! One returning missionary who had spent two years of fruitful labor in Europe was greeted by her mission pastor with, "Hi, Sally! How was Hawaii?"

One short-term missionary, after returning from a five-week ministry, was welcomed back at church with, "Bill! You're back! We thought you had backslid!" It was a blow for the returning missionary since it basically meant he wasn't being prayed for while on his mission.

There are real situations that may cause stress, but there are also imaginary ones that can be equally distressing: A family recently returned home to their church which had been kept informed about their mission. The husband said, "My best friends went sailing by, barely saying hello as if I had only been away for a long weekend. I was mortified! I was distraught!" His friends meant no harm. But rejection, whether real or imagined, can have equal consequences.

5) Linguistically

Your returning missionary has probably learned a second language—or at least some phrases. There are many languages of the world far more descriptive than English. He may try to express himself in our limited vocabulary and feel inadequate. Stress! He may have "forgotten" certain English words—which may be seen as humorous or inconsequential to most of his listeners. Stress! Some of his responses might automatically come out in his second language. Stress!

Further, colloquialisms and slang have changed. Teenagers of returning families might especially feel stressed by not knowing which words are in or out—or even if "in" and "out" are in or out! When you see a puzzled look on your returning friend's face, it may be the stress of not understanding American English!

6) Nationally, Politically

New leadership can bring new laws. Can you imagine your missionary leaving this country when the 55 mph was strictly enforced, then spending several years riding no faster than a bicycle can go only to return home to the maddening pace of our freeways today?

A visit to Iguazu Falls in southern Brazil can make the USA's Niagara Falls look like a miniature cascade! What happens to American nationalistic pride when we discover the technology of European television yields a much clearer picture than ours? Or when the mass transit systems of world-class cities make our freeway clog and smog a disgrace? Stress!

Having seen the other side of American foreign policies, your missionary's political outlook on this country may be affected. Possibly your returning worker found the government of his host country more to his liking. Singapore, for example, is a much quieter, gentler nation than the USA. Americans who live abroad sometimes feel that a socialized government offers more security to its citizens than does the pluralistic free enterprise of the US. As a returned worker simply reads a newspaper editorial about issues now facing his own society, he may be irritated with stress! And that is when you as a Re-entry Support specialist need to have your eyes and ears open!

7) Educationally

The formal and informal educational standards of the world vary. Missionary children may have for years been educated in home schooling or at a boarding school away from their parents. When the kids now have to go to a large public school, parents can understandably be concerned. The kids themselves can feel they are in a potentially devastating situation educationally as well as socially.

One girl, returning from the field to spend her seventh grade in a US junior high school, described her first day: "We circled the monstrous wood and brick building. We surged forward, carried irresistibly toward its mouth and stopped momentarily at its gaping door.... I was now in the monster's throat. I felt a downward, sinking feeling. I was being swallowed! The noise was like thunder.... I was alone in the blackness of that nightmare."

Actually, the description might fit what your returning missionaries and their children all might sense during the weeks and months of re-entry.

8) Spiritually

Your returning cross-cultural worker's life has concentrated on the salvation and discipling of the nations. He has sensed the very heartbeat of God pounding in his breast: "He is not willing that any perish, but that all come to repentance" (2 Peter 3:9). He has become disentangled with the affairs of this world "that he may please the One who has called him to be His soldier" (2 Timothy 2:4). He remembers the cry of the widow, the orphan, the lost and dying.

And now in bold, stark contrast, the demands of a "godless Christian" society surround him with stress. He is enjoying the pleasures of new conveniences at home in America, yet even that enjoyment can create feelings of bewilderment, anger, guilt and condemnation. The hurt is not only for himself; it is also for the hundreds of people he left back in his adopted country who need food and care and Bibles and Christian music and Bible studies and the multitude of other blessings of America.

Each of these areas—from professional to spiritual factors—is a stresspoint needing your re-entry support.

Re-entry Behavior Patterns
Generally, there are five different patterns of return behavior that could show up in your missionary friend. Four of them are dangerous. You want to be alert to their symptoms and help your friend process his feelings, working toward the expression of the fifth pattern. That is the one you want to facilitate.

1) Alienation
The cross-cultural worker comes home. His attitude of "I'm just going home!" has left him unprepared for what he is facing. He begins feeling very negative about his home culture. Not knowing how to handle what he sees and feels, he begins withdrawing.

He makes excuses rather than meeting people. "I don't have my slides together yet," he says. So he can't share with the home fellowship group. "The crowd at the baseball game would be too noisy," he argues. Three weeks later he is *still* "suffering from jet lag." These are the types of symptoms you must be on the lookout for.

They are shallow pretexts to hide his inner feelings.

He might internalize these feelings and sink further into this pattern of alienation. He may feel there is no one to talk to, no one who could possibly understand, no one to help him process his thoughts.

You can pull him out of that tailspin by inviting him to your home. Just the two of you—or three—is a small, safe number. Or visit some of his favorite spots together—a park, a beach, a restaurant. If he refuses all of this, get desperate! Just show up at his doorstep and *insist* on some fellowship! Get him talking about anything, just so he begins verbalizing his thoughts.

2) Condemnation

This person is also negative about his home culture. The areas of challenge seem to be overwhelming. He didn't realize people would be so unthinking. He can't understand *why* his pastor has no time for him. How *could* they be so unChristian! The pressure of his judgmental attitude increases, and he becomes explosive. Everyone he sees knows within minutes how inferior and lacking in spiritual gifts they are—so he thinks—because they are not involved in missions. He begins to condemn and criticize everything from the church pews to Mrs. O'Toole's new hair style.

Be blunt about his condemnations. Perhaps you could say, "My standing is in the righteousness of Christ. In whose are you standing?" Then let him talk to you. He, too, needs to verbalize all of his frustrations in the safe environment of a close friendship. Don't wait until he feels he must unload in the middle of a Sunday sermon.

3) Reversion

This person takes a hop, skip and a jump off the plane only to discover people aren't hopping, skipping and jumping any more. Yet he keeps trying to deny that any vital changes took place in him while he was gone, or in you who stayed home. He keeps trying to fit in to what was but no longer is.

This person is likely to jump right in to whatever task is put before him. And his unaware friends play right into this dilemma: "So glad you're back! We need a teacher for the sixth grade class!" "Great! When do I start?" Usher? "Yes, I will!" Lead worship on Wednesday night? "Sure!"

He will wake up one morning doubting his sanity. He has moved into the fast lane of American Christianity without allowing himself time to process the incredible changes his body, soul and spirit have endured.

4) The Ultimate Escape

Alienation, condemnation or reversion could lead your cross-cultural worker into a devastating scenario of the ultimate escape of suicide—figurative or actual.

The missionary went out to live and minister in a second culture. He had a good experience. Language was learned. Relationships were nurtured. Souls were saved. The church was strengthened.

He returns. He is *not* prepared for the changes at home. He tries to cope. He internalizes all his frustrations. Alienation whispers, "Nobody cares or understands. Forget them!" He argues with himself, "No, I have to get out and share a vision for the world among the church people." "But they are so ungodly," Condemnation thunders. "This isn't getting me anywhere," he yells back at himself. Reversion reasons, "Okay, let's just forget it. I was there. You were here. We're back together. No big deal!"

The whirlwind of emotions leaves him broken. He backs out of life—spiritually, mentally, emotionally, or finds the ultimate escape his only alternative.

If you see your returning friend falling into any one of these four behavior patterns, your help is needed!

The most vital immediate help you can give is to *listen!* Take the time to hear his heart, to share his experiences, to care about his feelings and burdens, to see his slides, to be there when he needs someone to talk and laugh and cry with.

The gala reunion parties are fine. But what about at three in the morning: You're awakened by the phone. At first you don't hear anyone on the line. Then you hear someone softly sobbing. You say, "Suzie, is that you?" There's a weak, hardly distinguishable, "Yes." You say, "I'll be right over!"

Let her say anything in the confidence of your friendship. Don't interject, "I know, yes, I understand." You probably don't! Just let her talk. Encourage her to keep talking by asking leading questions to explain something she has referred to. Ask often, "And how did you feel when that happened?" Affirm with "That must have been tough/terrifying/exciting/etc."

As stability returns to your friend, you can help her move into the fifth return behavior pattern—the only healthy one:

5) Integration
Helping your missionary integrate takes place on two levels: Immediate and long-range.

The Immediate
a) Be sure your workers are welcomed and picked up at the airport. Don't overwhelm them with half the church being there, but a good-sized group who will say, "We're glad you're home!" One church welcoming party came to the airport two days *after* the missionary had come home. Fortunately his parents had confirmed the correct day of his arrival and were there to meet him!

b) Have a place for them to stay. "And [Paul and Barnabas] *abode* with them there for a long time!" (Acts 14:28). It is noteworthy that of the twelve Greek words we translate "abide," the one used here is defined *to wear through by rubbing; to rub away!* In other words, their stay with the disciples in Antioch was of such a duration that all strangeness of relationship had come to be "rubbed away!" When you abide with someone, you know where the extra lightbulbs are stored. You aren't just camped out in the front hallway. Whether it is with friends, family, or in a place of their own, be sure to check with your missionaries before they return. Let them be prepared for the accommodations you are providing for them.

As a church recently brought home their first missionary family, the missions pastor said, "The washer and dryer are hooked up. The utilities are on, the refrigerator is stocked and the telephone is in service. I think we're ready!"

c) Have an immediate means of transportation for them—a borrowed car or a dependable, inexpensive one that can be sold when they return to the field. One returning woman said, "Not only did they have a comfortable, dependable car available for my three months home, but a gas credit card for my use!" It is important returning missionaries have some independence and the freedom to be mobile.

d) Provide meals for the first few days. Invite them over; bring food in; have their home stocked with some basic food supplies—and maybe a few treats. Take them out to their favorite restaurant.

But be sensitive. Don't make it difficult for them to say "No." Some missionaries have said, "I can hardly wait to get back to the field. I won't have to eat so much!"

e) Take them shopping. They may not know what

styles are fashionable. And they can look conspicuously out of place without even knowing it!

f) Perhaps they had complete medical check-ups just before leaving the field. If not, ask them if they would appreciate your making arrangements for doctor, dental and eye care visits—free or discounted or paid for by you or the church!

g) After an appropriate few days, have a get-together—perhaps a potluck dinner—so they can meet more people in a shorter time. A ladies' tea is great for the women to catch up and again feel a part of things. But again, be sensitive. They may want to spend most of their time alone for the first week or so.

Long Range Interaction

Help returned missionaries to *slowly* integrate their new identity and lifestyle into their new environment. They have the opportunity and challenge to be positive change agents—people who can purposefully help all of you back home to more and more see the world from God's perspective. Be open to their new ideas and ways of doing things.

Look for creative ways to help your missionary introduce global perspectives to your friends. What groups of people could you interest in hearing his report: Sunday service congregations? Sunday school classes? Home fellowships? Prayer groups? Public and private schools? Other churches' groups? Christian radio or TV? Secular radio or TV? A newspaper article? Is his story worth writing a book about?

Allow the creative genius of God to expand your thinking to other ways your missionaries can share their experiences. You can thereby facilitate a good debriefing for them. Paul and Barnabas, on their arrival in Antioch, were given the opportunity to "call the Church together and report to them all that God had done with them and how He had opened the door of faith to the Gentiles" (Acts 14:27).

Scripture further says of Paul and Barnabas that they stayed in Antioch for some time teaching and preaching the Word of the Lord (Acts 15:35). In other words, the time came when they picked up the ministry they had been involved in before going. In its time—if they are not returning to the field—taking up a ministry in the church would be a goal for your cross-cultural workers. This might possibly be in their area of previous ministry. But it is also possible that with their cross-cultural ministry experience, they would now be suited to further develop your church's involvement with internationals who live among you. Or to train new missionary recruits. Or to develop the many aspects of strong sending teams.

Personalizing Re-entry Support

There may be special re-entry concerns for various members of the family:

1) Husbands can use help.

As a family returns from the field, there are pressures and anxious feelings of responsibility on the husband as provider. Financial support may have dropped off because they aren't on the field now. Yet expenses are probably higher here at home.

Take the initiative in talking about money. Maybe you can help financially, maybe not. But you have helped by bringing the subject "out of the closet." Let him verbalize his family's needs. Even that may help to sort out priorities. And, then again, it might bring a totally new, Holy Spirit-inspired solution.

Go easy on this, but the time will come to help him talk about future plans. "What livelihood are you going to pursue?" "Are you planning to go back for more schooling?" "Back to the field?"

2) Behind every good man is a great wife!

On the field she probably played a much more active role in ministry than she will now. Be sure to allow opportunities for her to share. If this is not appropriate in your public gatherings, provide occasions in your living room. Often the wife in the missionary team bore enormous pressures in the balance of ministry and family affairs, and her needs to share are equally valid.

She is pleased with the fully-carpeted, three-bedroom, two-bath house the church rented for them. But she is at a loss as to how she is going to keep it clean! More often than not on the field she had a maid who had helped even with the cooking! Help her ease back into the skills of home-making. Be willing to help her with it for a time.

3) Missionary kids are ordinary kids.

Born to American parents but raised in Japan, Zaire, Cairo or Hong Kong, missionary kids (MKs) often don't know *where* they fit! America is their homeland, but it usually isn't their home.

A 14-year-old MK, after returning to the field from a year back in the US, wrote a ninth-grade essay titled, *What I Would Like to Tell the People Back Home.*

I want to answer a few questions I have been asked: No! We don't live in mud huts. No! We don't eat "foreign" food. It is very natural. MKs are not perfect. We're human and have faults and virtues like everybody else. When you subconsciously or otherwise treat us like we should be perfect, we get chewed out by you (who have *no right at all*) and then by our parents (who know better).

No! All MKs are not super brats. Those few who might act like it on furlough are probably trying to hide the culture shock they are going through. No!

Just because you're an MK doesn't mean you know your Bible any better than anyone else. All the time when we were on furlough, I was asked to quote Scripture or find something in the Bible I had never heard of. People were shocked and whispered behind their hands.

No! MKs don't go around barefoot and in rags. Mrs. X had seen a picture of me in a paint-spotted tee-shirt and cutoffs and assumed I didn't have anything better to wear. Please send money! The money sent to missionaries is never enough! Even though it often appears my folks aren't doing anything, they are! And our national friends will tell you so!

How can you support a returning MK? With all the tenderness and understanding and tact and wisdom and patience you would employ in being a re-entry support person for Mom or Dad use with a missionary kid.

4) Single and satisfied!

This book title might remind senders that singles may need special re-entry support. Few married people understand single ministry workers' special needs of being cared for. And few married couples realize the unintentional insensitivity and hurt hurled at single adults in even Christian circles.

Sometimes re-entry is harder for a single. At least family members have each other to talk with. Loneliness, perplexities, inability to cope with modern single relationships and the desire to get on with life can throw unmarried returned missionaries into quagmires of alienation and depression. You be there to draw them out! Be there to listen and serve as their "intensive care unit."

We are the Body of Christ. We are a community of believers. We need each other. May God challenge you to become part of a re-entry support team who are serving as senders!

A Case Study in Re-entry Support

One of the senders team we've been following in our case studies reports:

My wife Teri and I are the Core Group leaders of re-entry support for Lou and Sandy. The only experience we have regarding our responsibility was the short time Lou and Sandy were with us between their field training in Mexico and actually going to the Philippines. Because their time in Mexico was only three months, there didn't seem to be any of the major culture shock or stress problems. Still, when they came back from Mexico, we worked to make things as normal as possible for them. This was good practice for us!

Oddly enough the process started before they left for their field training. It began with a commitment on their part to keep those of us at home informed of what was going on in their lives in Mexico. We were kept up-to-date on prayer needs and trying situations in their training and in their "new" culture. We were told about the victories and the defeats. They kept us informed about their daughter Marlies and how she was growing and how all of them were adjusting to living with their host Mexican family. A key to this communication was that it was regular. We were "with them" as they progressed through the twelve weeks.

And that paid off. When they got back home they didn't have to feel pressured to condense or just hit the highlights of their experiences. And we hadn't missed so many of the little things that had contributed to who they now were. There was already a group of us who had "gone through it" with them, families with whom they could feel comfortable in rehashing some of their experiences. This detailed debriefing proved as important to them as it was informative to us.

Another aspect of their re-entry support was to attend to their physical needs. Before Lou and Sandy left for Mexico, they had sold most of their household things and had vacated their duplex. So there was a need for a place to stay for about seven weeks until their departure for the Philippines. Initially there was the chance that they might be able to house-sit for a family that was going to be out of town. As that hope faded and eventually disappeared, Teri and I felt that we should open our home to them. There were many things that contributed to our volunteering. We already knew them well and knew that our lifestyles were compatible. The Lord had blessed us with a large enough house that eight of us could live in it comfortably (including a kitchen large enough for both Teri and Sandy). There was an extra room that could be just for Lou and Sandy, while Marlies could stay in our daughter's room. And, most importantly, we all prayed about it and felt that the Lord was saying, "Yes!"

We were aware that a lot of people might want to spend some time with Lou and Sandy before they left for the Philippines. We planned a potluck reception after church their first Sunday home from Mexico.

Because we knew that there were quite a number of their friends that would like to share a meal or spend an evening with them, we decided to develop an appointment/social calendar so they could budget their time. We prepared a letter that was sent to the other Core Group members and all support members expressing Lou and Sandy's desire to spend time with those who wished to visit. It also explained their need for time to take care of unfinished business and to keep rested. The letter was sent out well in advance of their return. Teri acted as their appointment secretary. Lou gave us directions on how full to make their calendar and what days they already had planned for other things.

The rest was simply working with the people who called so that everyone could spend some time with them. It made things easier for us and even more enjoyable for Lou and Sandy when we could get a couple of families together at the same time. The letter proved to be successful in that Lou and Sandy were able to accomplish their three goals of visiting, doing business and resting.

The room we were able to provide for them was our den. We rearranged the furniture, brought in a bed and a chest of drawers and put a lock on the door so they could have privacy. They had their own keys to our house so they could come and go as they pleased. Even though they still had their own car, they were free to also use one of ours when they went in separate directions.

We have lived with other people at various times during our marriage, but I don't remember it ever being so tension-free. I think the major factor in this good living situation was that Lou and Sandy were doing exactly what God would have them do in preparing for the mission field and we as re-entry support team were doing exactly what God would have us do, He had prepared all of us to live together—for a while at least. And, as the widow from Zarephath who provided hospitality for Elijah found, the Spirit of God rested on our house.

Though our greater task will be when Lou and Sandy return on their furlough, we have learned a lot from this experience. Re-entry support doesn't begin when the cross-cultural worker returns home. It starts before they leave. It continues while they are gone. And *accelerates* when they return. While they are in the Philippines we are keeping in close contact with them so that when they return there will be a group of us who are not "cultural strangers" to them. We will be able to immediately relate with them as they begin their debriefing.

This then is the full circle of support you can offer to your cross-cultural worker as you express your love and concern for him while he is preparing to go, while he is on the field and when he returns home.

(In addition to the individual study below, see the **Group Leader's Guide** for session seven beginning on page 195.)

For Your Personal Involvement

• Though this aspect of missions life has been long neglected, articles are beginning to appear on the subject. From various missionary journals, collect and read as much as you can about re-entry.

• Talk with missionaries who are on furlough or those who have returned more permanently about the challenge of re-entry. But be prepared for some tears! Many missionaries, unless they have had a good Re-entry Support Team, have a lot of bottled-up emotions!

• As you listen to these people, try to identify symptoms of the first four re-entry behavior patterns.

• Write to the mission agencies of your cross-cultural workers. Ask them for the materials and useful ideas they recommend to help bring missionaries home.

• Write to other mission agencies and ask them for their materials and procedures. Learn all you can about this needy area of missionary support.

Action Steps

By the time you have read Chapter Seven, completed the *For Your Personal Involvement* section and participated in a discussion group, you should...

• Be able to decide if this is the area of support the Lord is directing you into.

• If it is, write to the missionary God has placed on your heart. Ask him if this is okay with him. Find out if there are others who have made this commitment to him. Begin networking responsibilities with the others.

• Four months before your cross-cultural worker comes home, send him material collected on re-entry that will help him prepare for his major transition.

• Multiply yourself. Share the material you collect and all you learn about re-entry with others. Make these people aware of this badly neglected area of missionary support.

Chapter Eight
Your Part in the Big Picture

"Be strong and very courageous that you may do it!"
Joshua 1:9

Why is it so crucial you and your fellowship gear up to serve as senders? Because most world-watchers believe God is beginning a surge of global activity in our times in which tens of thousands of new missionaries will be going to every people, tribe, tongue and nation. And every goer will need a solid team of senders.*

God is doing amazing things in our world. He's sending Eskimo missionaries to the Mongolians and European Gypsy believers to Madagascar and Argentina. He's shaking up Christian finances for His worldwide Cause. He's blasted through the Iron Curtain with effects felt even in Albania, that bastion of atheism. He's lighting fires of searing spiritual hunger in China, Latin America and Africa. He's raising a movement of excited disciples from around the world ready to go anywhere and do anything.

---

* Much of the material in this chapter is detailed in a brochure titled "Catch the Vision" and a study book *Catch the Vision 2000*. See "Resources," beginning page 201 for more information on how your fellowship can study the status of God's unchangeable global purpose.

Leaders in the world Christian community are

Leaders in the world Christian community are clarifying and focusing a vision for this decade:

Bill Bright, founder of Campus Crusade for Christ, says:

We live in the most dramatic moment in history, and I am trying personally—as well as Campus Crusade for Christ as a movement—to focus all of our activities on one great objective: the total saturation of the world by the year 2000.

[Campus Crusade's *New Life 2000* is] working together with millions of Christians from thousands of churches of all denominations and hundreds of other mission groups. It is our goal in *New Life 2000* to help present the Gospel to over six billion people prayerfully, anticipating at least one billion of those will receive Christ, several hundred thousand will be discipled, resulting in one million new churches being established.

Loren Cunningham, general director of Youth With A Mission, says:

We are in the most exciting time in all ages with regards to the fulfillment of Christ's Great Commission. By the year 2000 it is possible. Our annual growth rate of church planting is presently at more than eight percent per annum. We only need 11 percent per annum to allow us to place a living Christian fellowship—a local church—in every community in all the world as a witness.

In the past decade we have seen countries like Singapore have a ten percent increase of those who have seen Christ come into their lives as their personal Savior. Ten percent of Korea turned to Christ during the 1980s. Ten percent of Chile turned to Christ during the 1980s. Over ten percent in Indonesia—the largest Muslim country in the world. As we look throughout the world, particularly in Asia, Latin America and Africa, the 1980s was the greatest growth decade we have seen for the cause of completing the Great Commission.

We need action. We need commitment. It is time to commit. As Christians do so, we will see every people group reached with the Gospel.

Target 2000, a plan YWAM is promoting, is an effort on the part of the Body of Christ at large to plant a living, multiplying church in every unreached people group in the world by the year 2000.... It's a job that can be done.

Recently 1,302 participants from 50 nations gathered in Seoul, Korea for the Asia Missions Congress. In part, they affirmed: "We, the Christians and churches of Asia commit ourselves to make the Great Commission a focus and integral part of the life of every local church. We commit ourselves to educate and mobilize the entire membership of local congregations to send or go."

Mr. Seth Chansong, the General Secretary of the Evangelical Fellowship of Thailand (EFT) stated: "After hours of prayer, strategizing and seeking God's will, the EFT committee came up with four goals for the Thai church: 1) to have 3000 churches—one in each subdistrict by the year 2000; 2) to have 300,000 Christian believers; 3) to have 3000 Christian workers for at least one pastor in every church; and 4) to send out 30 missionaries overseas, supported by the Thai church."

Look What God is Doing
Let's take a World Christian view of what God is doing around the globe today. Here are a few highlights of this final decade of the 20th century—a period in which we will witness—according to many Christian leaders

worldwide—the greatest spiritual harvest the world has ever seen:

- The global fellowship of Bible believing Christians is growing at a rate of at least 70,000 people *every day.*
- 28,000 of those new believers live in the People's Republic of China. In 1950, when China closed to foreign missionaries, there were one million believers. Today, conservative estimates say there are well over 60 million.
- 20,000 of those new born saints live in Africa. That continent was 3% Christian in 1900 and is over 40% Christian today.
- 3,500 new churches are opening every week around the world.
- In 1900, Korea had no Protestant church; it was deemed "impossible to penetrate." Today Korea is 30% Christian with 7,000 churches in Seoul alone.
- In Indonesia, the percentage of Christians is so high the government won't print the statistic— which is probably nearing 25% of the population. The last accurate tally of Indonesian Christians reported that in 1979 more than two million Muslims turned to Christ!
- After 70 years of oppression in the Soviet Union, Christians number over 100 million—five times the number of the Communist Party at the height of its popularity and 36% of the population.
- The government of Papua New Guinea recently mandated Bible teaching in every school in the country.
- More Muslims in Iran have come to Christ since 1980 than in the previous 1000 years combined. Before Khomeni's revolution in 1979 there were about 2,000 Iranian believers. After years of intensi-

fied persecution, there are now more than 15,000.
- In AD 100, there were 360 nonChristians per true believer. Today the ratio is less than 7 to every believer as the initiative of the Holy Spirit continues to outstrip our most optimistic strategies!

(Most preceding statistics are interpretations of data provided by the Luasanne Statistical Task Force. See "Resources," beginning on page 201, for other statistical sources and update information.)

Where the church has been planted, it's growing like wildfire. And as it grows, it's reaching across language, racial and cultural barriers to unreached people groups. God has raised up Surinam missionaries to go to the Muslims of North Africa, Chinese believers to settle among unreached Tibetans, thousands of Indian evangelists to target the 2,000 unreached ethnic groups within India. The Good News is breaking loose worldwide!

And we see only the tip of the iceberg of our Heavenly Father's business these days. His perspective is infinitely deeper and broader.

To better understand and find our part as a sender in this awesome task of world evangelization, we must continually look for the bigger picture of God's purpose on earth in terms of bridging cultural distinctives and establishing strong, evangelizing churches where "Christ has not yet been preached" (Romans 15:20).

The Final Frontiers
What is the remaining task? What is the status of the Great Commission in today's world?

- Roughly half of the world's population—actually about 3.05 billion—live in reached people groups. This does not mean all these individuals are Christians; it simply means they live in people groups

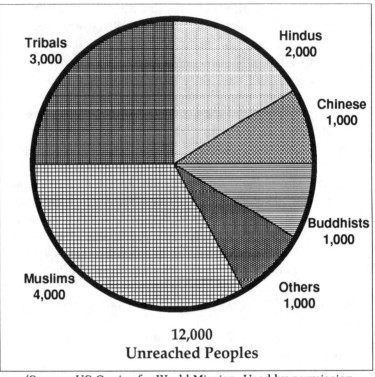

Tribals
3,000

Hindus
2,000

Chinese
1,000

Buddhists
1,000

Muslims
4,000

Others
1,000

12,000
Unreached Peoples

(Source: US Center for World Mission. Used by permission.
Graphic artist Richard Endo.)

where it's possible for them to respond to a clear
presentation of the Gospel from within their own
culture in their own language.
• There are about 12,000 reached people groups in
the world.
• In the rest of the world, about 2.2 billion people
live in unreached people groups.
• Currently there are about 12,000 unreached people groups.
• While about 1,000 of these unreached groups are
scattered among various world cultures, 11,000 of
them are mostly in five major cultural blocs:

❏ 4,000 unreached Muslim groups. Nearly a billion individuals are Muslims.

❏ 3,000 unreached tribal groups. About 140 million individuals are in these 3,000 groups.

❏ 2,000 unreached Hindu groups. These groups have a population of about 550 million individuals.

❏ 1,000 unreached Han Chinese groups. In these enclaves live 150 million individuals.

❏ 1,000 unreached Buddhist groups. About 275 million individuals are in these groups.

• These 12,000 groups are in about 3,000 clusters which have similar cultural characteristics such as having dialects of the same basic language.

• The unreached groups are mostly located geographically in what some scholars call "The 10/40 Window"—from West Africa across Asia between the latitudes of ten and forty degrees north.

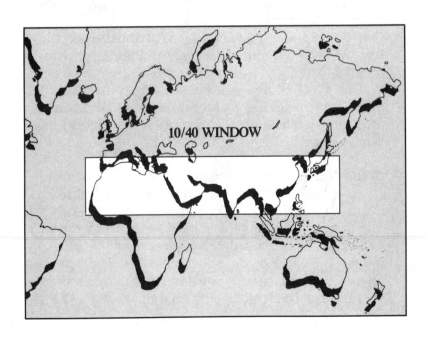

Within this 10/40 window are:

❏ most—not all, remember—of the world's un-reached peoples;

❏ two-thirds of the world's population, although only one-third of the earth's land area;

❏ the heart of the Islamic, Hindu and Buddhist religions;

❏ eight out of ten of the poorest of the world's poor, enduring the world's lowest quality of living.

Mission statesman Luis Bush, who is calling Christendom's attention to this region, also points out that the 10/40 Window "is a stronghold of Satan." He writes in the *AD2000 and Beyond* magazine (September 1990, page 7), "As the Christian presence has expanded around the world, it appears that those people living in the 10/40 Window have suffered not only hunger and a low quality of life compared to the rest of humanity, but have also been kept from the transforming, life-giving, community-changing power of the Gospel.... It appears that Satan has established a territorial stronghold with his forces to restrain the advance of the Gospel in this area."

The spiritual need staring at us from the 10/40 Window is a staggering picture to look at. Yet, when we grasp its significance, the next question we must ask is: What are we doing about it?

A Mission Renewal Movement

Historically, the modern movements to reach the ends of the earth with God's Blessing have occurred in waves. The first wave, championed by William Carey in the late 1700s, washed upon the seacoasts of the globe's continents. The second era, spearheaded by Hudson Taylor about 1865, thrust scores of bold and daring missionaries to the inland regions of the nations.

The Third Wave, responding to Cameron Townsend and Donald McGavran's call to go to the remaining culturally isolated "hidden" or "unreached peoples," is beginning to swell in this last decade before the year 2000.

Yet, as awareness of this surge is being broadcast, only 8% of the world's missionary force is currently deployed to these unreached people groups!

Manpower isn't the only area of imbalance in our attempts to make disciples of every nation. The world's believers spend .09% of their income on ministries to non-Christians in *reached* people groups, where a church movement has already been planted.

But the world's Christians spend only 0.01% on reaching the remaining unreached people groups. We know only too well where we put the other 99.9% of our money! (Statistics from *Our Globe and How To Reach It*, page 25. See "Resources," page 201.)

It is impossible to place statistics on effective prayer power that is being unleashed to support the work among unreached people groups. But given the general lack of knowledge of this final frontier and the basic Christian apathy to prayer, it would be safe to say that a very meager investment of prayer is being made.

But all of this is changing!

A Bold, Move Forward
As in New Testament times, today there are "Pauls" and "Timothys."

Though fewer in number, there are those who follow Paul's example of "going where Christ is not named." They have set bold, adventurous, aggressive goals to penetrate the final frontiers. "I have fully preached the Gospel in these parts...; I'm going to Spain"—which, in Paul's day, was the end of the earth! (See Romans 15.)

These 21st century, forward-thinking missionaries are taking the Mark 16 aspect of the Great Commission:

Go! Preach! to every person who has not heard the Good News in a culturally relevant context.

On the other hand, there is a second army of cross-cultural workers whose giftings lead them to follow the Matthew 28 command of the Great Commission: *Go! Teach!* Where daring evangelists of previous generations preached the Gospel of Peace there are today literally thousands of new "Macedonians" standing on the shores of their nations calling, "Come over and help us. Teach us the Word in such a way that we can teach others" (see 2 Timothy 2:2). It was Timothy, Titus and Erastus that Paul sent to "set in order the things that need attention and appoint elders in every city" (Titus 1:5).

Some people have suggested re-positioning the world's 150,000 missionaries from working in reached fields to target unreached peoples. But the work being done among reached peoples is crucial too. Established churches in areas of reached peoples need to be equipped, trained and motivated not only to evangelize their own people but to become sending bases to reach the unreached! Supporting the missionary workers and increasing our financing of this equipping ministry is definitely necessary to strengthen the new churches. These are the new wave of Third World missionaries.

For example, God is strategically using North American cross-cultural workers among Latin American reached peoples. These workers train and equip Latins to share Christ within their cultures and to go out by the hundreds as new missionaries to the frontiers— particularly to the Muslims of North Africa and the Middle East!

Shifting missionaries to target unreached peoples is not the answer.

To identify, challenge and mobilize bold, Pauline-thinking, world-class teams is the answer to the evangelization of the remaining 12,000 unreached people groups of the world. Good news: The task can be done!

We Have the Resources
When we think about 12,000 more people groups to reach, the task can seem discouraging—until we realize the resources God has entrusted to us.

For example, in AD100, there were about 12 unreached people groups for every one of the existing congregations of believers. Each congregation would have had to target 12 cultures in order to even begin discipling the nations! That must have been discouraging!

But in 1950, the ratio had shifted until there were about 33 congregations of true believers for each of the remaining unreached people groups in the world!

And today the odds are even more encouraging!

Congregations of Believers

1:12	1:5	1:1	10:1	33:1
A.D. 100	A.D. 1000	A.D. 1500	A.D. 1900	A.D. 1950

Unreached People Groups

(Source: The US Center for World Mission.)

For each remaining unreached people group, there are a total of 583 Bible-believing congregations (averaging 80 per church)!

What could happen if 583 churches banded together to become accountable for one unreached people group such as the Ewenki of China, the Engenni of Nigeria or the Bozos of Mali? What would be possible if they surveyed their memberships to put together a church-planting team, if they together provided the prayer power needed, if they pooled resources to provide the home-support of finances, encouragement, communication, logistics and re-entry?

What if just 100 churches committed themselves to reach one people group like the Bozos? What if just *ten* congregations determined to try out some functional unity enough to link up with a mission agency and reach that people? Or three or two? Or one— *your* church!

It's not only possible to reach the Bozos and the 11,999 other unreached groups, it is possible to field the necessary church-planting teams within a few years! Missiologists say that we can send church-planting teams to every one of the unreached groups within a seven-year period. To do it, we the whole church must:

  • identify 100,000 new missionaries,

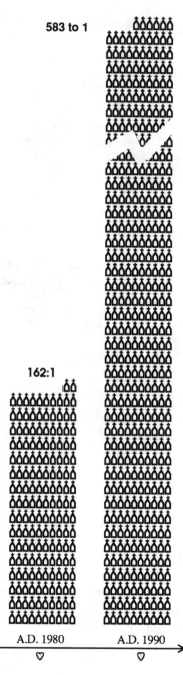

583 to 1

162:1

A.D. 1980   A.D. 1990

- double our missions giving, and
- pray more—at least a collective hour per day for each new missionary.

God will accomplish His purpose. The gates of hell that bar the unreached peoples of the world can't stand against His Church. At the end of time Christ will be exalted with the song: "Thou didst purchase for God with Thy blood men from every tribe and tongue and people and nation" (Revelation 5:9). So it's only a matter of *when* and through *whom.*

The fact is that we have more than enough resources in America alone to complete the task:

- Of the 70 million evangelicals in America, 17.5 million are aged 18-35. The 100,000 new missionaries needed are only half of 1% of the young believers available just in the USA.
- American evangelicals have a disposable annual income of about $850 billion. About one-fifth of 1% of that income—just $1.5 billion—would support the needed 12,000 church-planting teams.
- According to survey results, the prayer necessary would take only 2% of the time we evangelical Christians spend daily watching TV and shopping.

But this isn't a job for just Americans. With 430 million other believers worldwide, obviously the resources are available. For example, it is estimated that by the year 2000 there will be 83,500 Asian missionaries on the job. In 1980, Korean churches vowed to send 10,000 new missionaries by AD2000; but if they continue their growth rate of 725% per decade, they'll surpass that goal as of 1995!

There are more than 2000 plans operating right now that have as their goal the reaching of the entire world for Christ. Ninety-two of these plans are minutely detailed blueprints that specify how, with the resources we now have, every people, tribe, tongue and nation can have the opportunity to respond to the Gospel.

Many of the plans get specific about who will do what. For example, Larry Walker, the Southwest representative of the Association of Church Missions Committees, has been collaborating with several Southern California organizations to challenge churches to become accountable for 1,449 people groups! Basing his goal on the evangelical population of Southern California, Larry and mission enthusiasts are working to encourage churches to "adopt" unreached people groups.

We can establish a church movement in every remaining unreached people group, and then help those new believers to evangelize their own people group. It can be done! Will we be a part of it?

It Can Be Done. It Must Be Done.
We live in a critical hour. The resources are available. Decisive, aggressive action is demanded.

Yet, men have frozen to death lost in a blizzard just five feet from their front door! A whole generation of Israelis failed to "enter the land" because "we were in our sight as grasshoppers, and so we were in their sight" (Numbers 13:33).

Rather, we must be challenged by Paul's strong exhortation to the Church in Corinth: "Keep your eyes open for spiritual danger, stand firm in your faith, be courageous, be strong and let every thing you do be done in love" (1 Corinthians 16:13-14).

Imagine. It's a September morning in 1913. We're standing on a rise over the ocean in a balmy tropical breeze. We're looking south to the white waves of the Pacific crunching onto the smooth sand of Panama. We turn and look back to the unbelievable sacrifice of years and lives and funds represented in the huge ditch carved through the ridges and jungles from the Caribbean 40 miles to the north. We remember how French engineer Ferdinand de Lesseps set out in 1872 to finish the task of a canal across the isthmus of Panama. More than 20,000 men died before de Lesseps gave up just seven years later.

Now we've extended what the French began, and we're within sight of completing the entire project. We're standing on a hundred-yard chunk of rocks and dirt that still remains to be removed to complete the Panama Canal, one of the greatest engineering achievements in human history.

Chief engineer George Goethals strides up the slight rise and nods, "It's all here. We've got the dynamite to do it. The workers are ready. We've gone over the calculations again and again and figure we can cut our way through to the Pacific in about two days. We're ready. What do you say?"

As long as we're imagining, let's imagine you're the boss on this monumental project. What do you say?

Let's Do It!

When you see the end in sight on a huge project, it's not too tough to shout, "Let's finish the job!"

Now in the 1990s, the completion of the greatest project in history is within sight. The Church has the necessary information, the necessary resources and the necessary manpower to send church-planting teams to every remaining unreached people group on earth. The popular motto of "A Church for Every People by the Year 2000" isn't just a slogan anymore.

Blasting through the remaining tasks involved in this cosmic enterprise will not be easy; there will be blood, sweat, tears and casualties. But, in the 1890s words of the evangelist D.L. Moody, "It can be done. It must be done!"

In that same era of great anticipation for the completion of the task of world evangelization, toward the close of the last century, Bishop Thoburn of India, wrote:

"A century hence, with a world so revolutionized by technology and with the spread of the English language, the final conversion of all nations will no longer seem a far-off vision of a few enthusiasts, and the mention of a million converts will no longer startle timid or doubting Christians. We talk in hesitating tones about seeing a million converts now, but those who will fill our places a century hence will look out upon a scene where not a million converts but a million workers appear!" (See "Resources," page 201.)

When we learn of astonishing breakthroughs, let it build our faith! God can sweep whole peoples to Himself within a decade—or less, if He so chooses.

Books could be filled with global events in the breakneck rush of God's moving to uplift His Name among the nations. "Look among the nations," God shouted to Habakkuk. "Observe! Be astonished! Wonder! Because I am doing something in your days—you would not believe it if I told you" (Habakkuk 1:5).

Do we believe it? Astonishing wonders are happening before our very eyes. Each day's headlines read like the prophetic fulfillment of His Word.

More than 70,000 every day are trusting in Christ as Savior. The nations are being discipled. The Great Commission will be accomplished! The question: Will you be a part of it?

Full Circle
This exciting scenario—the possibility of being a part of the closure of His Great Plan of the Ages—brings us full circle back to you. You are as excited about "a church for every people by 2000" as any mission strategist who theorizes that it can be done. You are as zealous for a thriving church among the Bozos of Malias as any missionary who envisions going to them. You are as pas-

sionate about seeing the lost come to the Savior as any evangelist. But your zeal has been tempered with the knowledge from God that you are to stay right where you are, actively functioning in your local fellowship.

In this chapter we have focused our attention on the critical strategy of reaching the unreached. Let's super-impose this plan of "going where the Gospel has not been preached" over the grid of the six sending responsibilities of a support team. What additional activities for your involvement will this thrust provide for you?

Moral Support: Learn all you can about unreached people groups. Keep abreast of what is being done to develop and deploy the teams needed. When you hear of a person interested in going to the mission field, encourage him to focus on one of the two thrusts of cross-cultural attack: training Third World nationals to reach the unreached or taking the bold, Pauline drive to "Spain."

Read Joshua 1. Listen to God's continual encouragement to Joshua to "be strong and of a good courage" (v. 6). Again, "Be strong and very courageous..." (v. 7). Yet again, "Be strong and of a good courage; be not afraid, neither be discouraged..." (v. 9). And then, as the people followed God's example (v. 18), you shout the encouragement, "Be strong and of a good courage!" This is moral support at its best!

Logistics Support: If you hold some position (formal or informal) to influence the decision-makers of your church, encourage them to establish corporate mission policies that reflect the two-pronged thrust for training and frontier-focus through the kinds of cross-cultural workers and types of missions your church will support.

When missionary candidates come before your leadership seeking support, discern whether they are part of either a Pauline church-planting team ministry to an unreached people or a Timothy, teaching the Word to national leadership so they may go out to teach others or develop their church as a sending base. Better, look among your Body for the cross-cultural "parts" and mobilize them to become part of reaching the unreached.

Display prominently literature and posters that encourage reaching the unreached. On your church's map of the world, trace the 10/40 Window. Highlight any missionaries you have working in that area or that are training Third World nationals to go to that area. Border the Window with mirror striping. Let your church-goers see themselves involved in His world!

Financial Support: Until you have a specific friend moving into this type of cross-cultural ministry that you can financially support, consider directing your missionary offerings to organizations that are focusing on this massive plan of reaching the unreached. You can begin putting into practice the principles of "living more with less." You can submit yourself to the discipline of wartime austerity. You can encourage others to join you. These ideas can be effected on a personal and church level.

Prayer Support: To stretch your intercession to include this awesome task, prayerfully adopt an unreached people group. Learn about the people. Understand their lifestyle. Become aware of their religious practices. Pray knowledgeably for them. Gather a group around you for corporate prayer for the people, for the organization that will target the group, for the specific team that will enter their lives and for the churches that will send and support the team.

Pray for the mission leaders who are challenging the Body of Christ worldwide to participate in this task of world evangelization. Pray for the 2000 organizations that already have a program running to help complete the task.

Learn more about praying for unreached people groups through the *Operation World, Passports to the World* booklets on each country, colorful "People Profiles" on each unreached people group and the *Global Prayer Digest* (see "Resources," pages 200, 203, 204). Use these tools to help you focus your prayers on the unreached.

Spend an evening at your local library to look up information on the people group your missionary is working among—not just the political country he is in. Jot down findings that are significant to that people's needs, spiritual bondage and possible openings to the Gospel. If the group is one that is already reached and your missionary is equipping them for growth, find out how you can pray that they will become a strong sending base for their own missionaries!

Pray for your church to act more aggressively upon the challenge of reaching the unreached.

Communication Support: Contact organizations such as Friends of Turkey or Eastern European Outreach which can provide you with sample letters, Bibles, Bible correspondence material or tracts that you can send to pre-selected homes of unreached peoples in various countries (see "Resources," page 205).

Re-entry Support: Review our last chapter and remind yourself of the critical needs of missionaries returning from other cultures. Most totally unreached ethnic groups are especially different from Western culture, so re-entry stress is likely to be accentuated in these frontier mission workers.

But the experience they've gained and the unique information they've learned is particularly important for the home Church—for intelligent prayer and strategic planning. Welcome these returning workers into your home and your life. Let them share what they have been learning in your home group or at your church. Get them on a radio or TV talk show. Have their story written up in your local newspaper. Have them share at the schools and civic organizations. Give them that opportunity for debriefing and for spreading the news of what God is doing in these final hours of history!

(In addition to the individual study below, see the **Group Leader's Guide** for session eight beginning on page 197).

For Your Personal Involvement

• Read the story of Esther. (It's just a short book.) Pay particular attention to Mordecai's challenge to her when she was hesitant about going in to the king (Esther 4:13-14). As history records, Esther fit into God's plan and purpose for her. She truly was called to the kingdom for such an hour as that. Throughout the Word men and women fulfilled His will for their lives and found their place in God's Hall of Faith (Hebrews 11). Mordecai's question, reverberating down through the corridors of time, heard clearly by some generations, ignored by others, is sounding a challenge to you today—a challenge to recognize that you have been called to the Kingdom for an hour such as this! It is time to give serious, prayerful consideration: Has God placed a call on your life to serve as a sender?

• Reaching the unreached is such a fast-paced move of God that it is making yesterday's headlines look like ancient history. Because of this, contact some of the organizations listed in "Resources," page 200, to get current information on global breakthroughs among unreached peoples. Be prepared to share those highlights with your fellowship group.

Action Steps

This is it! A decision for personal involvement cannot be put off any longer! By the time you have read Chapter Eight, completed the *For Your Personal Involvement* section and participated in a discussion group, you should...

• Be able to decide if serving as a sender is the part of the Body of Christ that God has divinely established for you for right now. You might remember that in the very beginning we did say that if *not* serving as a sender is what God shows you by having read and studied this book, that is a good decision. Move on now to find and actively involve yourself in those "good deeds that He beforehand has determined for you to walk in, for you are His most finely crafted work of art created in Christ Jesus" for that purpose (Ephesians 2:10).

• If you do sense God's calling on your life to serve as a sender but still have not decided on one or another of the six sending responsibilities—or if you would like to do *everything,* go back over the *For Your Personal Involvement* sections to review each chapter. Find someone who knows you well with whom you can talk, particularly about the giftings and abilities that seem to be the qualifications for each category.

• If you have heard His confirmation and have found the one or more areas in which to serve as a sender, actively, aggressively pursue and develop this calling. Begin with the ideas given in this book, but don't be limited by them. Be creative. Expand your capacity to serve. Allow His genius to surge through you for, after all, "we have the mind of Christ" (1 Corinthians 2:16).

• Go back to the *For Your Personal Involvement* section of Chapter One, on page 24. If, when you were considering that chapter, you were not able to fill in the statement of the vitality of serving as a sender, reread those Scriptures and prayerfully complete that statement now.

• Multiply yourself. Having a clear purpose in your own heart and mind, actively seek others in your fellowship who will bind themselves with you in the task of serving as senders. Look for vibrant Christians who don't seem to "fit in" anywhere. It is quite possible they are looking for an opportunity like this. Share the six sending responsibilities with them.

For "Whosoever shall call upon the Name of the Lord will be saved. But how will they call upon Him if they have not believed in Him? And how can they believe in Him if they have never heard of Him? And how shall they hear of Him without someone to tell them? And how can anyone spread the Good News unless they are *sent?*" (Romans 10:13-15).

Epilogue

Serving as Senders barely scratches the surface of your potential involvement in caring for your cross-cultural workers.

Selected resources follow to give you more insight to this broad subject. But beyond all that you may acquire in your reading is the practical experience you will develop as you become involved in serving as a sender.

We would certainly appreciate hearing about your successes (and failures) as you put into practice the gifts of service God has given you. To God be all glory!

Neal and Yvonne Pirolo
Emmaus Road, International
7150 Tanner Court
San Diego CA 92111 USA
(619) 292-7020

Group Leader's Guide

Chapter One: The Need for Senders

After prayer, summarize the chapter:

❏ From Beth's story, what obviously was wrong?

• Neither she nor her pastor were aware of the critical issue of coming back home.

• Beth was not given (nor took) any opportunity to "debrief"—to verbalize the depth of her experiences.

• Beth may have had an overestimation of her role in missions involvement.

• Her friends didn't detect the symptoms of the trauma she was experiencing.

❏ Paul was a missionary statesman *par excellence.* Everything we do today to support our missionaries should find its foundation in Scripture.

❏ From Romans 10:13-15, it is clearly established that those who serve as senders share an equal responsibility and privilege with those who go.

❏ Psalm 139:14 says it succinctly: "I am fearfully and wonderfully made." The integrated yet extremely complex personality of your cross-cultural worker will be stripped of every "comfort zone" he has come to appreciate as he grapples with the various stages of his ministry experience. Because of this, he needs an active, knowledgeable and committed support team working with him while he is preparing to go, while he is on the field and when he returns home.

❏ What this book is encouraging every mission-minded church to do is being modeled by an average-sized church in Sacramento.

Go over the *For Your Personal Involvement* section:

❏ Help the group see the progression of Paul's linear logic establishing the *senders* as foundational to the goal of the salvation of the lost! It is true that the further one is away from the actual "action" of one praying the "sinner's prayer," the more difficult it is to feel a part of it. Perhaps a couple's experience at being far from the front lines could help illustrate:

We served for a time with Wycliffe Bible Translators in the jungles of Peru. My wife was assigned to keep inventory of the radio parts. For her, a fulltime "people-person," this took some discipline! By tracing the sequence from radio parts to the actual goal of Wycliffe, we were more able to rejoice in such a task. *Somebody* had to keep up the inventory of radio parts *so* the radio men could keep the airplane radios in repair *so* the pilots could fly the linguists to the villages *so* the linguists could translate the Bible *so* the indigenous people could have a culturally relevant presentation of the Gospel of Christ *so* they could put their trust in Him and be saved!

❏ Make sure the nine stages and the incidents in time that mark the transition from one to another are clearly understood.

❏ Read the six passages of Scripture that parallel the six support responsibilities. Make sure everyone sees the application of the Scripture.

❏ To help crush the pedestals of "cultural Christianity," share Christ's teachings on greatness in the Kingdom of God. Study Mark 10:35-45 and Matthew 18:1-4.

Pray for those who have committed themselves to a study of this book. Ask the Lord for clear insight to which area of support each should become committed. Or, if specific cross-cultural support is *not* their function in the Body of Christ, pray that that will be equally clear.

For Further Action

❑ Given the structure of your church, how can you proceed to elevate the vitality of the ministry of serving as senders?

❑ Do the missionaries your fellowship or you personally support know of these six areas of service available to them? You might want to survey your missionaries. Have them place the six support ministries in priority. Further, have them rate on some scale from "excellent" to "poor" how adequate they think their support is in each area. Careful! If they are honest with you, what they say may hurt!

Chapter Two, Moral Support

After prayer, summarize the chapter:

❑ From Scott and Jean's story:

• God is not the author of confusion, so obviously someone "heard" wrong.

• *Commitment* as senders is mandatory.

• Support coming from more than one fellowship is vital.

❑ From the biblical accounts:

• We see how common to man the *lack* of moral support is.

• It will take the wisdom of God and conscious effort to reverse the trend.

❑ From the foundation stones:

• Jesus is our example in Word and deed as the Chief Cornerstone.

• Do it simply—and simply do it!

• Moral support is a two-way street.
• Active listening is vital to moral support.
• *Called, counseled* and *commissioned* are watchwords for strong support.
❏ From building awareness:
• There are plenty of resources to encourage and challenge toward moral support.

Go over the *For Your Personal Involvement* section:
❏ Have several share their meditations on various translations of Matthew 12:20.
❏ Have a "teaser-length" (1-2 minute) book review of one or more of the books listed or others that have been read.
❏ Identify the kinds of people who can give solid moral support.
❏ Have several read their rewritten story.
❏ Discuss some of this world's philosophies—whether by bumper sticker, commercial jingles or other sources of input—that can distract us from giving moral support.

Pray for those who have made the commitment to actively encourage the Body of Christ. Pray for those who are still uncertain of their place in ministry.

For Further Action
❏ Contrast Joseph's initial response in Matthew 1:18-19 with Elizabeth's first words to Mary on her visit (Luke 1:39-45).
❏ Roleplay various non-supportive, then supportive responses to the following situations: A person is telling his parents that he thinks God wants him to go on a two-year mission trip.
❏ Roleplay: A person is telling his best friend that his parents are angry that he senses God wants him to go on a two-year mission venture.

❑ Roleplay: An assistant pastor is telling his pastor that a mission agency has invited him to go on a two-year mission venture.

❑ Design your own roleplay!

Chapter Three: Logistics Support

After prayer, summarize the chapter:

❑ From the story you can emphasize that nobody can do everything. But as everybody does something the job can get done!

❑ Both the Bible and growing mission agency practices are placing the responsibility of initiating the missions process on the local church.

• Identify the cross-cultural parts of your fellowship.

• Give them opportunity to exercise their gifts by being involved in a missions fellowship, by working with internationals in your home town and by going on a mini-mission.

• Check the accountability of the ministry with which they will work.

• Confirm their spiritual maturity and growth before they go, while they are gone, and when they come home.

• Establish good business practices governing all aspects of your missionary's affairs. If your missionary is going through a mission agency, you as his sending church still need to be aware of their policies and where you fit in.

❑ There are innumerable details that can be handled by a group of individuals.

• How should their material goods be handled?

• Are there family matters to be taken care of?

• What ministry needs can be met?

❑ The Body of Christ needs to care for its members showing diligence, concern for details, punctuality and sound business practices.

Go over the *For Your Personal Involvement* section:

❑ Discuss how to overcome the strong individualistic tendencies of our culture. How can we become more involved as the Body of Christ in each other's lives?

❑ Compile a master list from all the logistical needs each person wrote. Don't be overwhelmed! No one person will have all of these needs, but it emphasizes the diversity of needs and the vitality of Logistics Support.

Pray for those who have made a commitment to be a part of the Logistics Support Team for their missionary. Pray for those who have not yet made a commitment to any area of support.

For Further Action

❑ Consider the last missionary your church sent out. Who in the group knows which and to what degree the various logistical needs of that person are being met by your fellowship?

❑ Consider the internationals who live among us. What loss do they sense in not knowing how to establish all the logistics of "setting up" in a new culture. What can you do about it? Order *All Nations Dictionaries*, which are packed with Gospel messages in various definitions, to distribute as gifts to internationals in your area (see "Resources," page 204).

Chapter Four, Financial Support

After prayer, summarize the chapter:

❑ From the story you can emphasize God's faithfulness to supply financial support to ministries He directs. When senders diligently seek God for His direction in helping to financially support missionaries, He is faithful to provide the funds—possibly by very unusual methods!

❑ Typical methods of fund-raising do generate some working capital. But for the "long haul," more basic issues of financial management must be tapped:

Giving. The biblical principle of tithing yields to cheerful giving which grows in obedience so "there be equality." Wise giving carefully chooses who and what to support.

Lifestyle. Living more with less is an exciting, viable option in comparison to the shallow tenets of the Great American Dream.

Managing wealth on the field. By more carefully supporting economical, *effective* missionary strategy, you free up money for other decisive cross-cultural work.

Managing wealth back home. This is kinder and gentler to the environment as well as freeing up "megabucks" for missions!

Go over the *For Your Personal Involvement* section:

❑ From Scripture, discuss the philosophy of financial support Paul the Apostle seems to have adopted.

❑ Tithing is one principle of the Kingdom of God. It works!

❑ Encourage discussion surrounding the five questions on page 82. Avoid condemnation either of yourselves or others; however, allow the Holy Spirit His opportunity to convict in the area of *our* wealth.

❑ Media imput first *sells* us on our *needs,* then provides us with the plastic money to endebt us for life. Have someone share a vibrant testimony of victory over credit card buying.

Pray for those who have made a commitment to be a part of a missionary's Financial Support Team and for those who are still uncertain as to their personal involvement in serving as a sender.

For Further Action
❑ Consider sponsoring a Christian financial management seminar.

❑ Do a study on the financial accountability of the organizations with which your missionaries are working. (ACMC has material to help you ask the *right* questions (see "Resources," page 203).

❑ Do a study on the financial accountability of your missionaries.

Chapter Five, Prayer Support
After prayer, summarize the chapter:

❑ From Helen Mollenkof's story, it is clear that commitment to prayer is not to be lightly regarded; rather, it is a discipline of long-term obedience.

❑ Though the efficacy of prayer is a divine mystery, the practice of prayer is as clear as any Bible story.

❑ Prayer is the arena of spiritual warfare. Only the well-advised should enter there.

❑ The prayers of the Bible can serve as models for our prayers. These prayers provide for us the language and nature of petitions in line with the heart of God.

❑ Prayer with *fasting* is a powerful weapon in the spiritual warfare we are facing with our cross-cultural worker.

❑ "In-the-gap" praying is a level of intercession that demands a depth of commitment beyond the novice.

❑ "The harvest is plentiful; the laborers are few" is as true today as when Jesus spoke it. Therefore, "pray to the Lord of the harvest to send forth laborers" (Matthew 9:37-38).

❑ Pray that the Gospel, in a culturally-relevant context, will be presented to all peoples.

❑ Pray that the "strong man" will be bound.

❑ Pray for the coming of His Kingdom to the hearts

of all people.

Go over the *For Your Personal Involvement* section:

❑ Discuss the types of prayers the group has been used to praying.

❑ Discuss several model prayers of Jesus and other Bible characters that have been studied, and what differences the group anticipates in their praying now.

❑ Have someone who has prepared ahead of time give a book review of *God's Chosen Fast* (see "Resources," page 200).

❑ Have available the mailing addresses of your church's missionaries for those who are ready to make a commitment to their prayer support.

Pray for those who have made a commitment to be a part of a cross-cultural worker's Prayer Support Team. Pray for those who have yet to make a commitment to any area of support.

For Further Action

❑ Begin a mission prayer group, or increase awareness of the existing one(s).

❑ Give a more prominent visual place to the prayer requests of your missionaries by

• Posting letters on church bulletin board with prayer requests highlighted.

• Putting excerpts of those requests in the church bulletin each week or month.

• Requesting regular public congregational prayer for specific needs of your missionaries.

❑ Expand the vision of your church's outreach by using a world prayer guide such as the *Global Prayer Digest, Passport* booklets, "Unreached People Profiles" and *Operation World* (see "Resources," pages 200, 203, 204.)

❑ Prayer support is the most vital of the six areas.

• History tells of many who forged their way to

God's chosen fields of the world without *Moral Support*. But they got there.

• Having one or more friends back home handling all of the *Logistics Support* eases the mind of the cross-cultural worker. But they have survived without it.

• *Financial Support* does provide nicely for the worker's needs. But the belt can be tightened.

(And the two yet to be considered.)

• News from a far country provides great *Communication Support*. But loneliness can be handled.

• *Re-entry Support* certainly shores up the unstable as they come back home. But life goes on.

These five areas of support relate to the physical, emotional and psychological realms. Though the adjustments for lack of support in these areas are difficult, they can be made.

However, *Prayer Support* moves into the realm of the spiritual *where there is no adjustment for lack of support!* Therefore, make this issue the highest priority.

Chapter Six, Communication Support

After prayer, summarize the chapter:

❑ From the Paris missionary's story:

• God is merciful, but there is a better part of wisdom that says missionaries should get some good, practical training.

• Working with nationals enabled her to stay in the country.

• It was fortunate for her to see a positive example.

❑ From Mary's story:

• Even returning missionaries face difficulties that are helped by communication support.

• The encouragement of communication support

doesn't always take away the difficulty, but it sure helps your missionary through it.
❑ From the biblical writers:
• Make the communication real.
• Be personal.
• Even short letters should be written and sent.
• Communication support is for *their* benefit.
• Don't feel you have to say everything you know.
• Reminders are good.
• Sometimes your communication might be a God-inspired exhortation.
❑ Get everyone involved in letter writing.
❑ Be sure the content is worth reading.
❑ Use other methods of communication:
• Telephone, fax, telex, ham radio, photos, video, audiotapes, care packages, visits.

Go over the *For Your Personal Involvement* section:
   ❑ Have several share their highlighted letter of Paul. What was mundane in the letter—yet important enough to be included in Scripture? What did some of the other writers talk about?
   ❑ Make a list as the group relates the many different types of communication support missionaries have received.
   ❑ What have other churches found to be practical ways toward communication support?
   ❑ Compile a list of the resources within your group for communication support.

Pray for those who have made the commitment to be a part of a missionary's Communication Support Team. Pray for those who have not yet made a decision regarding any area of support.

For Further Action
□ Right now, let each one present have a half sheet of paper to write a personal note to your missionary. Gather them into one envelope and mail it—*tonight!*
□ Prepare a chart to show what time it is where your missionary is living and the best times to reach him by telephone.
□ Talk with the children's minister or Sunday school superintendent. Develop a plan for the children to write to missionary children in other countries.

Chapter Seven, Re-entry Support

After prayer, summarize the chapter:
□ From the seminary director's story:
• The devastation of this missionary's "crash" ripples out far beyond the circle of his immediate family.
• No doubt many factors beyond re-entry stress contributed to his "spiritual suicide." But *if* he had had a good Re-entry Support Team to unload on, what grief might have been averted!
□ From the Situation of Re-entry:
• Re-entry *shock* is the initial response and deals more with environmental changes your worker must face.
• Re-entry *stress* deals more with the deeper struggles of attitude and spiritual motivation that run contrary in the two cultures.
□ From the Challenge of Re-entry:
• Become very familiar with these eight areas. It is in one or more of these areas that you will sense some struggle in your returning cross-cultural worker.
• Know your worker well. Think beyond the examples given to specific issues that might frustrate him upon re-entry.

❑ From the Re-entry Behavior Patterns:
• Alienation, condemnation and reversion sometimes provide the degenerative spiral down to the
fourth, the ultimate escape. Be aware of these and if
you notice the signs, try to divert the returned missionary from this destruction.
• The focus of your re-entry program should be on
the fifth pattern: *Integration!*
• Integration is on two levels: The immediate needs
of living and long-range interaction.
• The most vital, immediate issue on either level is
the need for active listening.
• The Re-entry Support Team must provide opportunities for debriefing. This is as much for your worker's benefit as it is for the edification of the group
listening.
• In time, slowly help your worker become involved
in some meaningful level of ministry.
• Consider the specific needs of the various family
members or single adult.

Go over the *For Your Personal Involvement* section.
❑ Review any articles on the subject of re-entry.
❑ Hear the real stories of re-entry given by returned
missionaries.
❑ Develop a plan for educating the Body on this area
of support.

Pray for those who have made the commitment to be a
part of their missionary's Re-entry Support Team. Pray
for those who have not yet made a decision regarding
any area of support.

For Further Action
❑ Obtain information that various international cor-
porations use to bring their employees home. Incorporate transferable material to your program of re-entry.

❑ In the opening chapter of this book, we related Beth's story in which she was so distraught by her lack of re-entry support that she chose to take her own life. By God's mercy, that plan was thwarted. Unfortunately, there are other less final but equally serious forms of suicide that may require professional help. If it appears that a returning missionary is not responding to the care you are able to provide, there are groups equipped to help.

One highly recommended organization in the US is Link Care Center. Contact Link Care Center, 1734 West Shaw Avenue, Fresno CA 93711, phone 209/439-5920.

❑ There may be members of your fellowship who would like to participate in a broader hospitality ministry to missionaries. Makahiki Ministries is dedicated to providing short-term hospitality housing around the world for missionaries. To find out how you can help missionaries find a respite from their hectic pace, contact Makahiki Ministries, P.O. Box 575, Kailua HI 96734 USA.

Also, most mission agencies are looking for senders willing to open their homes in hospitality to returning missionaries. One such agency is Wycliffe Bible Translators, P.O. Box 2727, Huntington Beach CA 92647 USA.

Chapter Eight,
Your Part in the Big Picture
After prayer, summarize the chapter:

❑ Leaders in the global Christian community are taking bold, aggressive steps to mobilize and deploy thousands of new missionaries to reach the unreached.

❑ God is doing a mighty work among the nations. Yet about half of the earth's population lives beyond a simple, culturally relevant presentation of the Gospel.

❏   Most of the world's 12,000 unreached people groups—in 3000 clusters—mostly live in a geographic region called the 10/40 Window.

❏   Until recently, very little has been done to target these people. In fact, today only about 8% of the world's missionary force is working among unreached peoples.

❏   They can be reached by a two-pronged attack:

1) Send thousands of "Timothys" to teach Third World nationals the Word in such a way that they will teach others. God is sovereignly raising up thousands of new Third World nationals to go as missionaries to the unreached.

2) Identify, mobilize, train and deploy thousands of "Pauline-bold" teams to penetrate these final frontiers of unreached peoples.

❏   The Christian community has the resources to see this mission accomplished by the year 2000.

❏   As part of this worldwide move, we can actively serve as senders in the six areas of support as they relate to reaching the unreached.

Go over the *For Your Personal Involvement* section:

❏   Focus on that most critical question Mordecai gave to Esther: "Who knows but that for an hour such as this, you have been called to the kingdom?" Relate and discuss other Scriptures that lay a responsibility for action on us to participate in God's Great Commission (Genesis 12:1-3; Isaiah 6:8; John 20:21; Matthew 28:18-20; Mark 16:15; James 1:22).

Pray as various ones share global breakthroughs on what God is doing to reach every people.

For Further Action

❏   Contact the Adopt-A-People Clearinghouse (1605 Elizabeth St., Pasadena CA 91104 USA) on how you can take responsibility before God for an unreached people group.

Resources

Books for Further Study

These books are available from 1) your local Christian bookstore, 2) the publisher listed, or 3) William Carey Library (PO Box 40129, Pasadena CA 91114 USA, 818/798-0819).

Chapter One, The Need for Senders
A Mind for Missions, Paul Borthwick (NavPress)
Student Mission Power, (William Carey Library)
Culture Shock, Myron Loss (Light and Life Press)

Chapter Two, Moral Support
From Jerusalem to Irian Jaya: A Biographical History
    of Christian Missions, Ruth Tucker (Zondervan)
Shadow of the Almighty: The Life and Testament of
    Jim Elliot, Elisabeth Elliot (Harper & Row)
Chasing the Dragon, Jackie Pullinger (Hodder &
    Stoughton)
Bruchko, Bruce Olson (Creation House)
Vanya, Myrna Grant (Creation House)
Tortured for His Faith, Haralan Popov (Zondervan)
I Dared to Call Him Father, Bilquis Sheikh (Chosen
    Books)
Anointed for Burial, Todd and DeAnn Burke (Logos
    International)
A Distant Grief, F. Kefa Sempangi (Regal Books)
The Jesus Style, Gayle D. Erwin (Ronald N. Haynes
    Publishers)
To Understand Each Other, Paul Tournier
    (Westminster John Knox)
Eternity in Their Hearts, Don Richardson (Regal
    Books)

Chapter Three, Logistics Support
  Income Tax Law, B. J. Worth (Worth Tax Service)
Chapter Four, Financial Support
  Living More With Less, Doris Janzen Longacre
    (Herald Press)
  Out of the Salt Shaker and into the World, Rebecca
    Pippert (InterVarsity Press)
  Tentmakers Speak Out, Don Hamilton (TMQ
    Research)
  The Support-Raising Handbook, Brian Rust and
    Barry McLeish (InterVarsity Press)
  "*Making Yours a Wartime, Not a Peacetime,
    Lifestyle*," Ralph D. Winter (William Carey Library)
Chapter Five, Prayer Support
  Touch the World Through Prayer, Wesley Duewel
    (Zondervan)
  Destined for the Throne, Paul Billheimer (Bethany
    House Publishers, Christian Literature Crusade)
  This Present Darkness, Frank Piretti (Crossway
    Books)
  Piercing the Darkness, Frank Piretti (Crossway
    Books)
  The Discovery of Genesis, C.H. Kang and Ethel R.
    Nelson (Concordia)
  God's Chosen Fast, Arthur Wallis (Christian
    Literature Crusade)
  Operation World, Patrick J. Johnstone (STL)
Chapter Six, Communication Support
  We Really Do Need to Listen, Reuben Welch (Impact
    Books)
Chapter Seven, Re-entry Support
  Honorably Wounded, Marjory Foyle (MARC Europe)
Chapter Eight, Your Part in the Big Picture
  Destination 2000, Bob Sjogren (Frontiers)
  Our Globe and How to Reach It, David Barrett and
    Todd Johnson (New Hope)

The Christless Nations, J.M. Thoburn (Hunt &
Eaton)
Catch the Vision 2000, Bill & Amy Stearns (Bethany
House Publishers)
Asian Church Today, Alfred C. H. Yeo, editor (EFA)

Mission Vision Resources

Check with your church, denominational or mission
agency for mission vision resources.

The following "generic" resources can be ordered (except where noted) by phoning toll-free in the USA 1-800-
MISSION to the "Target Earth" mission resource order line
on-campus at the US Center for World Mission, 1605 Elizabeth St., Pasadena CA 91104 USA.

Resources marked with an asterisk (*) are designed for
easy customization by your denomination or organization.

Step One
Encourage your fellowship to *catch the vision:*
• Simply set out *"Catch the Vision" brochures.
  10-packs—$3

• Wear an **Adopt-A-People T-shirt or sweatshirt**
  and answer people's questions about it. $10, $20

• Post on a bulletin board a *Mission Prayer Map**
  listing an amazing amount of information on the
  harvest field—including the 72 largest unreached
  people groups. $7.95
     An explanatory 10-minute video on the various
  features of the map equips you to use it as a
  teaching tool. Or simply show it to a group as a
  world-awareness program. $11.95

* Customizable. Call 1-800-MISSION for details.

- Display in a conspicuous place an ***Unreached Peoples Poster** with its jam-packed information on the global task we're facing as the harvest force. $5.95

- Offer to insert an unreached-people-focused **FrontierScan bulletin insert** in your newsletter or bulletin once a month. $3 per 100

- Encourage your fellowship's leaders to present ***A Sunday for the World,** a complete one-day festival of the amazing breakthroughs and challenges in what God is doing worldwide. Includes Sunday school lessons and activities for every age group, sermon outlines, fact sheets, overhead formats and promotional visuals, bulletin note-taking forms, family take-home prayer guides for unreached peoples, small-group follow-up Bible studies and more! $8.95

Step Two
Equip your fellowship to *build the vision:*
- Provide Bible study curriculum for Sunday School classes, home Bible study groups and training hours.

    Use the intensive ***Destination 2000* video study course** for a 12-week study program. $107.50 for the 10 videos. *Destination 2000* audio series and books are also available.

    Study through the ***Catch the Vision 2000* book and *Group Leader's Guide**. $6.95 per book; $8.95 per Group Leader's Guide.

- Provide up-to-the-minute input for your mission fellowships and mission committee sessions:

    Make sure everyone on your mission committee gets **Mission Frontiers**, the monthly, insight-packed bulletin of the US Center for World Mission. Subscriptions are just $4 per year!

    Study in group sessions this *Serving As Senders* book. $5.85 per book includes the group study guide; quantity discounts available.

    View **WorldView Videos of unreached peoples.** Each quarter a video cassette arrives with three 5-minute profiles of unreached peoples—with a study and prayer guide for each group. Twelve unreached people videos on four cassettes yearly. Give a subscription to your fellowship and subscribe yourself. $88 per year

    Evaluate mission agencies with whom you would consider working with the **Mission Agency Inventory** available through ACMC, P.O. Box ACMC, Wheaton IL 60189 USA.

- Host a *Perspectives on the World Christian Movement* course at your church. For college credit or audit this 20-session curriculum dramatically impacts each participant with a vision for personal involvement in missions. Contact the Perspectives Study Office for details (818/398-2125).

- Equip your fellowship's prayer groups and shut-in prayer warriors with global fuel for prayer:

    Pray from the monthly *Passports to the World* **booklets**. Each 34-page book is a colorful, information-packed profile on a specific country and its peoples. Each comes with a powerful prayer intercession guide. Give a subscription to your fellowship and subscribe yourself. $25.20 per year

* Customizable. Call 1-800-MISSION for details.

Pray from the ***Unreached People Prayer Cards**. Each profile with full-color photographs is a large greeting-card-sized focus on the culture and prayer points of an unreached people. A new Prayer Card every month. Give a subscription to your fellowship and subscribe yourself. $14.50 per year

Get your fellowship into the daily habit of prayer for the unreached with the monthly ***Global Prayer Digest**. Order bulk shipments for your group; subscribe yourself at just $6 per year.

Study **Prepare for Battle: Lessons in Spiritual Warfare**, a 9-hour video or audio program (see page 206 for details).

* Provide as reference tools for your church library:
   Target Earth, the most colorful mission-focused atlas and commentary you can find! $24.95
   Kids for the World, a catalog of the best in children's mission resources. $11.95

Step Three
Challenge your fellowship to *act* on the vision:
* Distribute the **All Nations Dictionary** to internationals in your area. The full-sized dictionary is packed with scriptural definitions of words like *grace, God, heaven, sin* and more that add up to an excitingly clear Gospel presentation! $6 each; quantity discounts available.

* "Adopt" an unreached people. Introduce the Adopt-A-People concept with the **Adopt-A-People**

Advocate Kit. The kit includes an explanatory video, handouts, overhead transparencies, fact sheets and more. $49

Use the ***Adopt-A-People Video or Slide Presentation** even apart from an Adovocate Kit presentation. $9.95 for video; $40 for slide presentation

• Order **Stepping Out**, a $4.50 magazine-style encyclopedia of short-term mission issues. Stock your library with annual issues of **Lifetime Memories—Short-term Opportunities** from more than 100 mission agencies! $5

• Through these organizations have direct correspondence contact with people in restricted countries:

Friends of Turkey, P.O. Box 3098, Grand Junction CO 81502

Eastern European Outreach, P.O. Box 983, Sun City CA 92381

Open Doors with Brother Andrew, P.O. Box 25101, Santa Ana CA 92799.

Help your fellowship catch, build & act on the vision!
Call 1-800-MISSION
(All prices are subject to change without notice.)

Ministries Available Through Emmaus Road, International

Video/Audio Training Tapes

Prepare for Battle: Lessons in Spiritual Warfare—This 9-hour video or audio training tapes program comes with 19 pages of student notes and assignments and a study guide for groups or individuals.

Building Your Support Team—This 2-hour video training tape is the counterpart to this book, instructing the missionary in how to develop relationships in the six areas of support.

Solutions to Culture Stress—This 4-hour video training tape helps prepare a short-term missionary for the culture stress of going and returning home.

Publications

Critical Issues in Cross-Cultural Ministry is a bimonthly bulletin on vital missions topics. The themes of the issues revolve on a two-year cycle. Available back issues include:

Series I: *Mobilizing Your Church*
Series II: *For Those Who Go*
Series III: *Serving As Senders*
Series IV: *Internationals Who Live Among Us*

Seminars

Nothing GOOD Just Happens! Seminar—This is an intense, 21-hour seminar to train church missions leadership in how to mobilize their fellowship in cross-cultural outreach ministry.

For Those Who Go Seminar—The sessions of this seminar help the potential cross-cultural worker look beyond the "romanticism" of missions and to deal with some very practical issues of going.

Serving as Senders Seminar—The lessons of this book are presented in a 6-hour seminar format.

ACTS Training Courses

ACTS Team Orientation—2-10 hours of cultural, interpersonal relationship and spiritual warfare training for short-term teams.

ACTS Boot Camp—One week of cultural, interpersonal relationship and spiritual warfare training for those serving up to six months.

ACTS 29 Training Course—An intensive 12-week immersion in a second culture to learn how to live and minister in other cultures. The courses include cultural adaptation, language acquisition, interpersonal relationships, spiritual warfare and unculturating the Gospel and teachings of Christ. This field training incorporates classroom study and community experience with living in the home of a national.

Speakers Bureau

Neal and Yvonne Pirolo are available as speakers on a variety of subjects, all challenging to a personal involvement in cross-cultural outreach ministry.

For more information on these or other developing resources to equip you and your church for cross-cultural ministry, contact:

Emmaus Road, International
7150 Tanner Court
San Diego CA 92111 USA
619/292-7020